GO *(together)* and MAKE

SEVEN STEPPING STONES TO EVERYDAY MISSION

By Mark van den Steenhoven

Jacolien van den Steenhoven-Janse

Sharon Earl

**GO (*together*) and MAKE
Seven Stepping Stones
to a Missional Lifestyle**

www.stepping-stones.nl
E-mail: info@stepping-stones.nl

Published by GX Books
Editor: Bob Rognlien
Cover Design: Tim Bergren, Bergren Design

First Edition, 2018, Second Edition 2024

TABLE OF CONTENTS

Stepping Stone Two
Living a Balanced and Integrated Lifestyle

Stepping Stone Five
Forming a Spiritual Family

INTRODUCTION AND ACKNOWLEDGEMENTS

Introduction

We believe that every 'ordinary' Christian can live an integrated missional lifestyle so that he or she can have daily impact in their context. It is for this reason, we support, equip and encourage 'ordinary' Christians to live 'extraordinary' lives. This can be done as part of a 'Discipleship Immersion' (life on life discipleship) or as part of a coaching group via video conference calls.

GO (*together*) and MAKE is written for those who want to grow as a disciple themselves, who are already discipling others or have a longing to do so. The aim is to see disciples who make disciples who make disciples. Our experience is that often the material you read is about concepts or 'big pictures'. What we have tried to do is to write down the so-called 'nitty gritty', more practical things, of a missional lifestyle. Most of the content isn't new or our own ideas. It is an accumulation of experience, information and a few years of immersion in the culture of missional discipleship.

We, Mark and Jacolien, had the privilege to move to Sheffield (United Kingdom) to be part of 3DM Europe, a training organization, and Network Church Sheffield. We started a missional household with Sharon Earl who had been immersed in the discipleship culture in Sheffield for twenty years. We offered people the opportunity to live with or close to us and to be part of our missional community in Sheffield and to experience living a missional lifestyle. This is what we've called a 'Discipleship Immersion Year'.

What we've learned about and practiced regarding missional discipleship was birthed and developed in Sheffield by Mike and Sally Breen (and others) and is written down in several books. 'Building a Discipling Culture' is one of them. It explains some fundamental tools of discipleship, developed within 3DM. At the end of this book you'll find a list of titles which were helpful in our journey of learning to live a missional lifestyle ourselves.

For the past few years, 3DM Europe has been the central training organization for churches in Europe wanting to learn about this DNA of discipleship and mission. Kairos Connexion is the national network for England and Wales that has taken on the responsibility for developing this growing relational network. 3DM North America is the expression of this movement in Canada and America.

This a practical book which guides you through the different phases of growing yourself as a disciple and building a missional lifestyle. You'll find questions to reflect on and to discuss. The best way to learn is together with others and a practitioner who has experience with living a missional lifestyle. You don't have to read it in chronological order, although it is good to start with Stepping Stone One, which is foundational.

Acknowledgements

We want to thank Rich and Anna Robinson who initially invited us to come over to Sheffield and to be part of their 'oikos' and the 3DM Europe team. Thanks to John and Liz Lovell, investors within the missional movement, for their wisdom, encouragement, investment in us and friendship. Liz has also been a great help with editing. Thanks to Jo Dring for her friendship and proofreading. Thanks to Cath Livesey for helping us to grow in listening to God. We thank St. Thomas Philadelphia and the wider family of Network Church Sheffield for being our spiritual home for the last few years. Thanks to Peter and Ann Findley for their leadership. Thanks to Charlotte, Robin, Sam, Rachel and Giles for journeying together. It was a privilege to be part of the same Huddle.

Thanks to Bob Rognlien, Dick Weidenheft, Jenna Frisk, and Greg Grunau for help in editing the book for a North American audience. Thanks to Tim Bergren for redesigning the cover for this North American edition.

We hope that this workbook will be beneficial for your personal journey of following Jesus and when you're discipling others.

STEPPING STONE ONE

THE BASICS OF MISSIONAL DISCIPLESHIP

MISSIONAL DISCIPLESHIP

Hearing the combination of missional and discipleship you could think why add the word missional. The adjective missional refers to the sending part of discipleship. We think it is important to emphasise that discipleship should include the sending part, because that isn't always obvious when we talk about discipleship. There could be a tendency to separate evangelism from the discipleship proces. By doing that there will be a distinction between making disciples, bringing people to Christ, and discipleship, growing people up in Christ, but we need both. As you will read in this Chapter the missional part of discipleship isn't optional.

THE MEANING OF DISCIPLESHIP

By discipleship we mean the process of making disciples. The Greek word for 'disciple' is *mathētēs* and refers generally to a pupil, student or apprentice. A disciple is a 'learner', but being a disciple is not only about gaining information or agreeing to a set of theological beliefs, it's also about imitating the teacher's life, adopting his values and reproducing his life. Basically a disciple wants to become like his teacher. A Christian disciple is a person who is determined to follow Jesus Christ, with the desire to learn from Him, become like Him, and live according to His example.

When Jesus invited the twelve to follow him He invited them to be with Him, to know, enjoy and become like Him. Following in Jesus' time was not only hearing and learning his teaching but following in the literal sense, living his lifestyle and imitating that. This is the same for us. Jesus invites us to be with Him, to know Him, intimately and to follow him along the path of

discipleship.

So discipleship is the process of being with Jesus, knowing Him and becoming more and more like Him - both in character and competence

Discipleship can be described as simply following the person and patterns of Jesus. Ann Spangler and Lois Tverberg who have done a lot of research about the Jewish context of Jesus life, write: "The mission of a rabbi was to become a living example of what it means to apply God's word to one's life. A disciple apprenticed himself to a rabbi because the rabbi had saturated (soaked) his life with Scripture and had become a true follower of God. The disciple sought to study the text, not only of Scripture but of the rabbi's life, for it was there that he would learn how to live out the Torah. Even more than acquiring his master's knowledge, he wanted to acquire his master's character, his internal grasp of God's law."[1]

All we need to do is - be on this journey. To have chosen a lifestyle set to pursue these things. This is a journey from our inner being to the outer world. This doesn't mean that we need to be perfect to get started. We are living examples - not perfect examples.

Living and learning from Jesus, we move from servants to friends who have received everything He has received from the Father. "I no longer call you servants, because a servant does not know his master's business. Instead, I have called you friends, for everything that I learned from my Father I have made known to you." (John 15:15).

From observers of his works to participants. From fearful men who are able to lay down their lives for Him. We are called to be people who are living with Him, listening to the Father, full of the spirit, able to come into his throne room of grace and receive all that He has for us, to be people who can do the same and even more than Jesus did (John 14:12).

---

1   Ann Spangler and Lois Tverberg, *Sitting at the Feet of Rabbi Jesus*, Kindle Loc 556

If we are growing in this, we are carriers or representatives of the Kingdom - "Because the Kingdom of God is within you" (Luke 17:21). We do have good news to share. If we are not disciples, our mission is empty words but if we are living with Jesus and learning from Him we will be living authentic powerful lives and be able to partner with Him in calling others into this life.

Question:

Take a minute to think about what stood out for you? It can be completely new or it can be an important reminder. If you are reading this together, be ready to share it with someone in the group.

THE MISSION OF GOD, JESUS AND THE CHURCH

By mission we mean the mission of God (Missio Dei) and therefore the Mission of the Church. *Missio Dei* is a Latin Christian theological term that can be translated as the "mission of God," or the "sending of God." Darrell Guder, an American missiologist writes: "We have come to see that mission is not merely an activity of the church. Rather mission is the result of God's initiative, rooted in God's purpose to restore and heal creation. Mission means 'sending' and it is the central, biblical theme describing the purpose of God's action in human history."[2]

Sometimes people think that mission is the same as evangelism, but mission is much broader. Bob and Mary Hopkins give us a helpful distinction:
Mission is the totality of God's activity to restore His order (Kingdom) to the whole of His creation
Evangelism is that part which seeks or results in the restoration of God's right relationship with humanity as the good news of Jesus (gospel) is both told and lived out.[3]

To fully understand the mission of God we can look at the life of Jesus. Jesus himself made clear what his mission on earth was:
"The Spirit of the Lord is upon me, because he has anointed me to proclaim good news to the poor. He has sent me to proclaim liberty to the captives and recovering of sight to the blind, to set at liberty those who are oppressed, to proclaim the year of the Lord's favor." (Luke 4:18-19).
"For the Son of Man has come to seek and to save what was lost" (Luke 19:10).

These two verses show us the heart of who Jesus is and what his mission is about. Bringing people back into a relationship with God and remove every blockage which

---

2   Darrell L. Guder. *Missional Church: A Vision for the Sending of the Church in North America.* p4

3   *Evangelism Strategies*, Hopkins, loc 333

can hold people back. Guder writes: "God's mission continued with the incarnation of Jesus. And then in the sending of the Spirit to call forth and empower the church as the witness to God's good news in Jesus Christ. It continues today in the worldwide witness of churches in every culture. We have learned to speak of God as a "missionary God". Thus we have learned to understand the church as a "sent people". "As the Father has sent me, so I send you" (John 20:21)[4]

In the same way Jesus was sent by the Father, He sent out his followers to continue His mission: When Jesus had called the Twelve together, He gave them power and authority to drive out all demons and to cure diseases, and He sent them out to proclaim the kingdom of God and to heal the sick. (Luke 9:1-2)

In summary, we see in Luke 4:18-19 that Jesus explained his mission and in Luke 9:1-2 that He delegates it to his disciples:

Luke 4:18-19
"The Spirit of the Lord is upon me, because he has anointed me to proclaim good news to the poor. He has sent me to proclaim liberty to the captives and recovering of sight to the blind, to set at liberty those who are oppressed, to proclaim the year of the Lord's favor."

Luke 9:1-2
"When Jesus had called the Twelve together, he gave them power and authority to drive out all demons and to cure diseases, and he sent them out to proclaim the kingdom of God and to heal the sick."

And in Matthew we can read the commissioning of making disciples:"Then Jesus came to them and said, "All authority in heaven and on earth has been given to me. Therefore go and make disciples of all nations, baptizing them in the name of the Father and of the Son and of the Holy Spirit, and teaching them to obey everything I have commanded you. And surely I am

with you always, to the very end of the age." (Matthew 28:18-20)

Jesus sent his inner core of disciples into the world for the purpose of expanding the Kingdom of God and making more disciples. These new followers of Jesus would not only believe in him, but also would obey all the commands Jesus gave to his first disciples. The second generation of disciples were to make more disciples, who would make more disciples, who would make more disciples, and so forth until all nations are filled with disciples of Jesus.

This Commissioning is Twofold
"Love each other. Just as I have loved you, you should love each other. By this everyone will know that you are my disciples, if you love one another." (John 13:34-35). "Go and announce . . . that the Kingdom of Heaven is near. Heal the sick, raise the dead, cure those with leprosy, and cast out demons. Give as freely as you have received!" (Matthew 10:7-8)

Question:
In what way do you feel part of this bigger mission of God? What is your challenge regarding mission?

---

4   Darrell L. Guder. Missional Church: A Vision for the Sending of the Church in North America. p4

MISSIONAL DISCIPLESHIP AND LIFESTYLE

Every follower of Jesus is called to be a disciple and we are all sent to make disciples. It's not only for 'professional' Christians, like pastors, ministers, missionaries, etc.

The tendency is that when we commit to serving the Lord as ordinary Christians we simply focus our efforts on serving in the context of church. We join the worship team or children ministry or lead a Bible study group etc etc ... while these are all valuable they are not taking on our calling as missional disciples.
In Matthew 5 Jesus says that we are the light of the world. "You are the light of the world. A town built on a hill cannot be hidden. Neither do people light a lamp and put it under a bowl. Instead they put it on its stand, and it gives light to everyone in the house. In the same way, let your light shine before others, that they may see your good deeds and glorify your Father in heaven." (Matthew 5:14-16)

Living as a missional disciple is not simply a matter of taking on new ministries in church - we need to take on the lifestyle of mission in our everyday life. This is for every Christian, we can participate in God's mission in the world at work, at school, at the gym, in volunteer work, in financial priorities, at the dentist etc. It is who we are not what we do and therefore integrated into the ordinary things of life. We don't turn it on and off. It is seeing every part of your life as an opportunity for mission.

Mission isn't about an activity, a role or job, it's a lifestyle!

Question:
How integrated is mission into your ordinary life as a disciple? Score yourself on a scale of 1-10

MISSIONAL FAMILY

We were never designed to be alone. The first thing that God said about Adam was that it would not be good for him to be alone. In Genesis 1:18 God said: "It is not good for the man to be alone. I will make a helper suitable for him."

God himself is a trinity, or in other words, a community. In Genesis 1:26 God said: "Let us make mankind in our image, in our likeness, so that they may rule over the fish in the sea and the birds in the sky, over the livestock and all the wild animals, and over all the creatures that move along the ground." Also in the new testament we read about God as a trinity. "For there are three that bear record in heaven, the Father, the Word, and the Holy Ghost: and these three are one." (1 John 5:7)
Jesus came to the earth to join and embrace our

humanity and be part of a human family and community. "The Word became flesh and blood, and moved into the neighborhood." (John 1:14 MSG)

We can't do mission on our own. When Jesus sent his first disciples into the world, he sent them as a community or family, not as a bunch of isolated individuals. Through the Bible we see that most of the time the disciples worked together. One of the main principles for this is given by Jesus in John 13: 34-35, which we mentioned earlier: "Love one another. As I have loved you, so you must love one another. By this everyone will know that you are my disciples, if you love one another."

In Acts 2 we read about how the first disciples lived their lives in community and as a family.
"They devoted themselves to the apostles' teaching and to fellowship, to the breaking of bread and to prayer. Everyone was filled with awe at the many wonders and signs performed by the apostles. All the believers were together and had everything in common. They sold property and possessions to give to anyone who had need. Every day they continued to meet together in the temple courts. They broke bread in their homes and ate together with glad and sincere hearts, praising God and enjoying the favor of all the people. And the Lord added to their number daily those who were being saved." (Acts 2: 42-47). Here we find the word 'oikos' used to refer to the homes and households.

Households were essentially extended families which functioned together with a common purpose.[5] A missional family is a group of people with whom you live a missional lifestyle. This family is not the same as a nuclear family which consists of a mom, a dad and 2.4 kids - it's more like an extended family who are on a mission together.

---

5   Mike Breen. *Leading Missional Communities*, p.4

18

CHAPTER 2

COVENANT RELATIONSHIPS AND KINGDOM RESPONSIBILITIES

In Chapter 1 we've looked at missional discipleship, basically answering the question why we're doing what we're doing as Stepping-Stones. We've seen that God is on a mission to restore his creation and that He wants us to join him. The tendency is thinking that being a Christian has to do with doing things. But when we look at Jesus' life, the first thing He did was to invite his disciples into a relationship with him - to be with him. "He appointed twelve that they might be with him and that he might send them out to preach" (Mark 3:14).

Not only do we see Jesus doing that, but through the whole Bible we see that God is inviting us into a relationship with Him and others. We call this Covenant.

After the relationship is established, Jesus started to train his disciples to do the same things He was doing. When we know Jesus, there is a responsibility to step out in obedience and to represent God in this world. This is about doing. We call this Kingdom.

WHAT IS COVENANT?

A covenant (Hebrew 'berith', Greek 'diatheke') is a legal agreement between two or more parties and it means 'becoming' or 'being one'. God calls us to live in a covenant relationship with Him. This covenant relationship defines our identity. Because God initiated this relationship we don't have to do anything.

Covenant - the way in which the Bible describes and defines relationship: first our relationship with God and then our relationship with everyone else.[6]

WHAT IS KINGDOM?

Our Covenant relationship gives us our identity and security of the Father's love and all the resources of heaven (including the indwelling of the Holy Spirit). Our Kingdom responsibility urges us to change the world and it is about what we do.

Kingdom - the way in which the Bible describes and defines responsibility: first our responsibility to represent God to the people we know and then to everyone else.[7]

Covenant Before Kingdom

If we were asked what it means to be a Christian some of us would put it all in terms of covenant: to be a Christian is to have a relationship with God through Jesus. But others would use language of the Kingdom: to be a Christian is to live for him and join in his mission in the world. In reality, we cannot have a relationship with God and not join in his mission in the world; mission is not optional. Equally, we can only be effective in his mission in the world if we are in relationship with him. Therefore it's important to start with our Covenant relationship with God before we're taking our Kingdom responsibilities.

Once we know these two principles, we discover that the Bible is full of Covenant and Kingdom. We just mentioned Mark 3:14. "He appointed twelve that they might be with him - this is Covenant Identity- and that He might send them out to preach" - this is Kingdom task responsibility.

Matthew 4:19: "Follow Me (Covenant), and I will make you fishers of men (Kingdom)."

---

6 Mike Breen, *Covenant and Kingdom*, XV

7 Mike Breen, *Covenant and Kingdom*, XVi

And in Matthew 6:9-13 when Jesus taught his disciples to pray He started with 'Our Father' (Covenant). Jesus called God 'Abba' which means 'dad' and He included his disciples in this family relationship. The second phrase of our Lords prayer is 'Your Kingdom come', which is the prayer we bring as sons and daughters who are declaring our obedience to the Father, our responsibility to represent him in the world as good news (Kingdom).

Question:
Most people tend to focus more on either Covenant or Kingdom. What is your tendency?

THE COVENANT AND KINGDOM TRIANGLES

These triangles are simple visual tools that help us understand and remember. First the Covenant triangles (one based on relationship and another one based on religion) and then the Kingdom triangle.

The Covenant Triangle - Based on Religion

If you are not sure about your identity, it may be hard to see God as a loving Father. You start to 'earn' your identity by being obedient to the law. We are then living from religion, when the things we're doing are the foundation of our identity - we try to do things from our own strength, not relying on the power of the Holy Spirit.

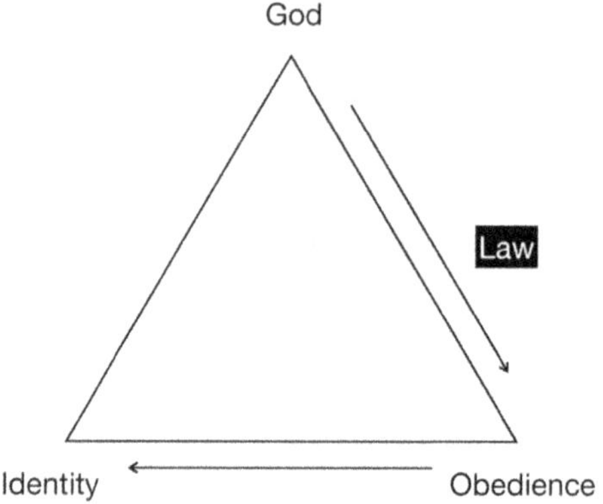

The Covenant Triangle - Based on Relationship

Father - Through the sacrifice of Jesus and our faith in Him, our relationship with God the Father has been restored. We receive identity, security and belonging. "See what great love the Father has lavished on us, that we should be called children of God! And that is what we are!" (1 John 3:1) "This is love: not that we loved God, but that he loved us and sent his Son as an atoning sacrifice for our sins." (1 John 4:10)

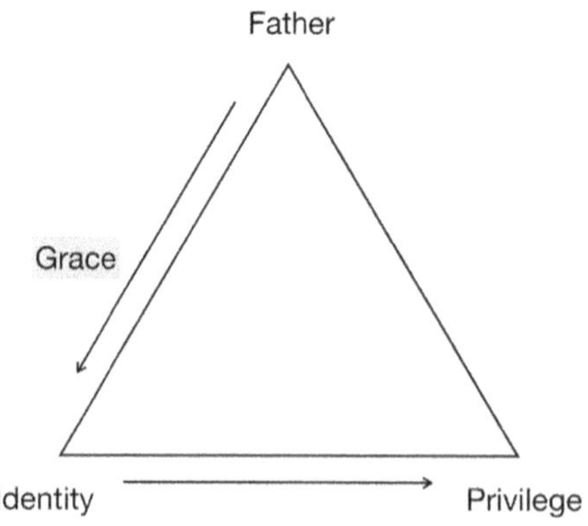

Identity - By being part of this family we receive a new identity. We become beloved sons and daughters of the most high. It's by grace that we receive our new identity. This new identity gives us our security.

Before Jesus started his ministry He was confirmed by the Father for who He was. This confirmation is about being and not doing.

"As soon as Jesus was baptized, he went up out of the water. At that moment heaven was opened, and he saw the Spirit of God descending like a dove and alighting on him. And a voice from heaven said, 'This is my Son, whom I love; with him I am well pleased.'" (Matthew 3: 16-17)

2) We also received the Holy Spirit.
"Because you are his sons, God sent the Spirit of his Son into our hearts, the Spirit who calls out, 'Abba, Father.' So you are no longer a slave, but God's child; and since you are his child, God has made you also an heir. "(Galatians 4:6-7)

"And this hope will not lead to disappointment. For we know how dearly God loves us, because he has given us the Holy Spirit to fill our hearts with his love." (Romans 5:5)

"...and he has identified us as his own by placing the Holy Spirit In our hearts as the first instalment that guarantees everything he has promised us." (2 Corinthians 1:22)

"For when we brought you the Good News, it was not only with words but also with power, for the Holy Spirit gave you full assurance that what we said was true. And you know of our concern for you from the way we lived when we were with you." (1 Thessalonians 1:5)

Privilege - As we simply start to live out our new identity fuelled/empowered by the indwelling of the Holy Spirit we realize it is a privilege to join what the Father is doing. We simply start to live out who we are. "You are my friends if you do what I command. I no longer call you servants, because a servant does not know his master's business. Instead, I have called you friends, for everything that I learned from my Father I have made known to you." (John 15:14-15)

With Covenant we mean that we live from this relationship with God, which is the foundation of our identity.

Questions:
Do you recognize these triangles in your life? Can you give an example of when you tried 'to earn' your identity?

Can you think of barriers that make it hard to embrace your identity in Christ? (ungodly beliefs)

The Kingdom Triangle

King - God is not only our Father, but also King. Which means that He reigns over all things. This means that there's no higher authority.

God as Father gives us our identity - who we are: sons and daughters.

God as King gives us the authority - what we need to do - our Kingdom responsibilities.

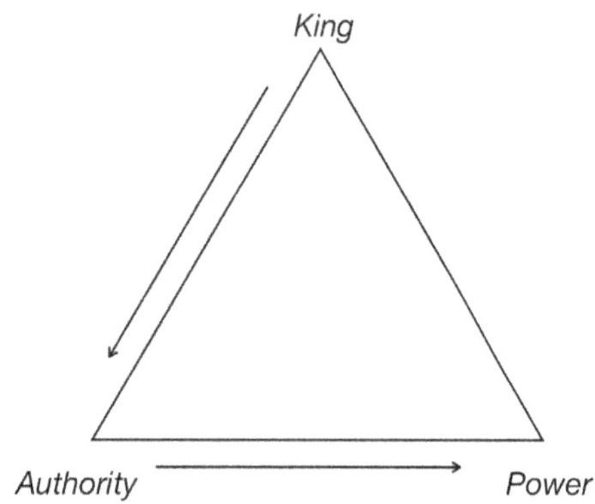

Authority - In Matthew 28:18-20 we read: "All authority in heaven and on earth has been given to me. Therefore go and make disciples of all nations, baptizing them in the name of the Father and of the Son and of the Holy Spirit, and teaching them to obey everything I have commanded you. And surely I am with you always, to the very end of the age." God has given this authority to Jesus.
And in Luke 10:19 we see that Jesus gave this authority to his disciples so that they can represent Him. "I have given you authority to trample on snakes and scorpions and to overcome all the power of the enemy; nothing will harm you." The word in greek for authority is 'exousia' which means: power to act.

Power - Not only do we have the authority, God also gives the power we need to act through his Holy Spirit. As we receive the revelation of our authority we can receive the power that we need to do the things Jesus commissioned us to do. In Acts 1:8 we read: "But you will receive power when the Holy Spirit comes on you; and you will be my witnesses in Jerusalem, and in all Judea and Samaria, and to the ends of the earth." and in Luke 9:1-2 we read: He called the twelve together, and gave them power and authority over all the demons and to heal diseases. And He sent them out to proclaim the kingdom of God and to perform healing.

Jesus' Use of Authority and Power

It's important to understand that Jesus didn't act randomly or on His own. He always went to his Father to listen and acted in line with what God was saying and doing. It's crucial to listen to God first. This is what we mean when we say that Covenant comes before Kingdom. We need to know that it always starts with our relationship with God and to listen to Him before we step out and do things in the Kingdom.

"Jesus answered and was saying to them, "Truly, truly, I say to you, the Son can do nothing of Himself, unless it is something He sees the Father doing; for whatever the Father does, these things the Son also does in like manner. "For the Father loves the Son, and shows Him all things that He Himself is doing; and the Father will show Him greater works than these, so that you will marvel." (John 5:19-20)

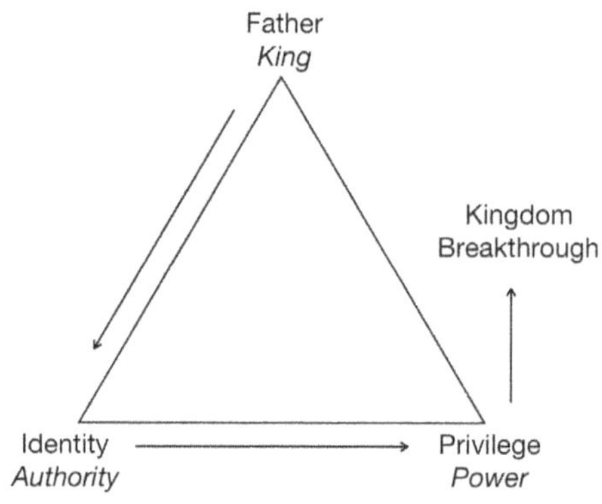

Questions:

Are you (really) aware of your authority given by Jesus?

What do you think when you hear 'power'? (healing, deliverance, speaking truth, etc etc)

Covenant comes before Kingdom. It always starts with our relationship with God and listening to Him before we step out and doing things in the Kingdom. - Is listening to God a familiar concept to you?

If it is, how do you listen to God?

CHAPTER 3

IDENTITY AND DESTINY

In Chapter 2 we've seen that our new identity is key and it has two sides. One side defines who we are (Covenant) and the other defines our responsibility to represent God in the world (Kingdom).

Once we are living in our true identity as sons and daughters we can begin to discover our destiny. One part of that is already known: we are called to rule. Similar to Willem-Alexander in the Netherlands and King Charles in England we are born to rule. As soon as they were born, their destiny was obvious: to become the king of their nation. The destiny we all share is to demonstrate God's nature to the world. To be representatives of His Kingdom.

The other part is that each of us is uniquely wired and gifted for specific good works God has called us to. "For we are God's handiwork, created in Christ Jesus to do good works, which God prepared in advance for us to do." (Ephesians 2:10). We have our own specific part to play. In Chapter 15 and 16 we'll take a look at 'Vision' and 'Calling.'

WALKING IN OUR IDENTITY TO SEE KINGDOM BREAKTHROUGH

Right now we want to take a closer look at our identity. The key topic in Chapter two about Covenant and Kingdom is our identity in Christ. When we want to see Kingdom breakthrough, by which we mean God's power and authority influencing the world around us and changing individuals, whole communities, countries and continents, we need to realize that we can never be ministers of this breakthrough if we are not walking in our true identity. If we aren't sure about who we are in Christ then it's hard to experience and see Kingdom breakthrough. Therefore we first need an internal breakthrough so that we realize who we are.

This principle is woven throughout the whole of the story of the people of God:

- It was in the Garden of Eden that we first gave up our identity as blessed, fruitful, ruling offspring of God (Genesis 1:28), because of our unbelief, greed and ambition (Genesis 3:1-6). As a result satan stepped into the position of ruler of this world that had been originally given to Adam (John 12:30-34).
- Abram needed to hear his new identity as Abraham (father of a mighty nation) before he could trust God for a son and could be fruitful he still had to let go of his desire to fix it himself and trust God and obey him.
- It was not until Gideon heard his true identity as a mighty warrior that he was able to throw off fear and lead the people into victory.
- David was anointed as king and then had years to get the breakthrough of walking as child of God, depending on him and fighting with lions and bears before the giant. He went deep in his journey of worship and learned patience and wisdom in Saul's court. It was only after all this internal work that he was able to step into his authority and win great victories and bring in the golden age for the people of Israel.
- Jesus is the perfect example of winning the internal battle before He was led by the power of the spirit in the desert and there was tempted by the devil. He succeeded where we had failed.

THE GIFT OF GRACE

So disconnection from our Godly identity leads to sin which holds us back in stepping out in God's Kingdom. Sin literally means "falling short of the mark". This disconnection with our true identity means we are missing the richness of the path He has set out for us. We need to throw off all that holds us back and trips us up so we can run the race God has for us (Hebrews 12:1, Philippians 3:13).

We need to deal with our internal issues first. Often this isn't a quick fix, but an ongoing process. In the Chapter about Covenant and Kingdom we've seen that by grace we are children of God which gives us our identity. In Ephesians 2:8-9 we read: "For by grace you have been saved through faith; and that not of yourselves, it is the gift of God; not as a result of works, so that no one may boast."

TEMPTATIONS TO PROVE OUR IDENTITY AND REACH OUR DESTINY

In Chapter 2 we've seen that before Jesus started with his ministry his identity was affirmed by his Father. But another thing happened before He started his ministry. The Holy Spirit leads him into the desert for 40 days. In Matthew 4:1-11 we can read the story of Jesus in the desert:

"Then Jesus was led by the Spirit into the wilderness to be tempted by the devil. After fasting forty days and forty nights, he was hungry. The tempter came to him and said, "If you are the Son of God, tell these stones to become bread." Jesus answered, "It is written: 'Man shall not live on bread alone, but on every word that comes from the mouth of God." Then the devil took him to the holy city and had him stand on the highest point of the temple. "If you are the Son of God," he said, "throw yourself down. For it is written: "He will command his angels concerning you, and they will lift you up in their hands, so that you will not strike your foot against a stone.'"Jesus answered him, "It is also written: 'Do not put the Lord your God to the test.' Again, the devil took him to a very high mountain and showed him all the kingdoms of the world and their splendour." All this I will give you," he said, "if you will bow down and worship me." Jesus said to him, "Away from me, Satan! For it is written: 'Worship the Lord your God, and serve him only.' " Then the devil left him, and angels came and attended him."

This temptation by the devil was two-fold: he asked Jesus to prove himself IF He is the son of God, which is about His identity, and he offered him a shortcut to reach His destiny. Basically saying that Jesus can't trust God and should take matters into His own hands. Let's take a closer look:

We can see three areas where the enemy tries to tempt Jesus and us as well:
1. Tell these stones to become bread - Appetite
2. Jump from the temple - Affirmation/Approval
3. Receive all the kingdoms of the world - Ambition

If we are not walking in this true identity we are going to fall short of God's Glory - being ensnared by sin as we try to create our own identity independent of him. We will be tempted by Approval, Ambition and/or Appetite.

No longer secure as children we will be dogged by a need to receive approval from others. This leads to vanity, pride, resentment, jealousy, dishonesty, etc. No longer dependent on his filling - we will become self protecting, greedy, fearful, materialistic, hedonistic, political, manipulative, etc. No longer following Him and his goals - we will become ambitious, stubborn, self seeking, self righteous, judgmental, dominant, passive, etc

1. Temptation of Appetite
Jesus was tempted to throw away His right to walk securely in God's abundant provision trusting him to provide. He would be tempted to feed his appetite to provide for himself.
For us this looks like a temptation to find our own security and provision. To provide our own comfort. We call this the temptation of APPETITE.
Underlying fear: We want to be secure, so the underlying fear is fear of lack, pain, sorrow emptiness or fear of poverty. So we seek to provide for ourselves through physical comfort and through people and things around us.
Basic lie: there is probably not enough for me, I'm vulnerable and alone. I have to care for myself.
Basic emotion: Anxiety

2. Temptation of Affirmation/Approval

Jesus was tempted to throw away his right to live as a confident Son of his faithful heavenly Father, trusting his Father to affirm who He was rather than having to prove himself.

For us the temptation is to try to prove that we are worthy and unique. We call this the temptation of APPROVAL.

Underlying fear: We want to be accepted and the underlying fear is rejection. We don't think we're worthy, therefore we feel shame for who we are. So we desperately try to behave and create a persona, to succeed so we are acceptable to people around us. We are caught up in our own image rather than celebrating the goodness of our amazing Father.

Basic lie: I'm not worthy or valuable. I need people's approval to feel ok about myself.

Basic emotion: Shame.

3. Temptation of Ambition

Jesus was tempted to throw away His right to be a representative of His Father, the Lord Almighty. Trusting God that it is Him who make us significant, not what we accomplish or possess.

For us this is the temptation to try to create our own life to change the world ourselves and thus be truly empowered alive and justified. We call this the temptation of AMBITION

Underlying fear: We want to be significant, so the underlying fear is fear of being nothing, of failing to be in control, of failing to get it right. We think that our accomplishments will give us the power/authority we crave instead of trusting God.

Basic lie: I have to make my own destiny. I have to change things by my own efforts, I need to be in control to be ok.

Basic emotion: Guilt.

Questions:

Which of these temptations do you recognize when you face a period of wilderness?

In what way are you tempted to fix it yourself?

HOW TO DEAL WITH THESE?

Jesus answered with quoting the Bible and that is what we need to do.

Appetite

Truth: I have the Holy Spirit living in me right now. Therefore I'm connected to the resources of heaven. He is my constant companion and guide and the source of all good things.

1 Corinthians 3:16: "Do you not know that you are a temple of God and that the Spirit of God dwells in you?"

Galatians 5:22-23: "But the fruit of the Spirit is love, joy, peace, forbearance, kindness, goodness, faithfulness, gentleness and self-control. Against such things there is no law."

Philippians 4:19: "And my God will meet all your needs according to the riches of his glory in Christ Jesus."

Our calling: to be vessels of his presence and ministering his generosity to others.

Approval

Truth: I'm of huge value to my Father who loves me, made me and treasures me. His voice is the only one that matters.

1 John 3:1: "See what great love the Father has lavished on us, that we should be called children of God! And that is what we are! The reason the world does not know us is that it did not know him."

Our calling: to be noble children of his kingdom who honour others and invite them into their royal identity.

Ambition

Truth: Jesus is the great warrior King, my protector, the prince of Peace and my Righteousness. I can have life, peace and grace as I submit to him. It's his rule (not mine). He is building his church and I'm privileged to join in, this is my destiny.

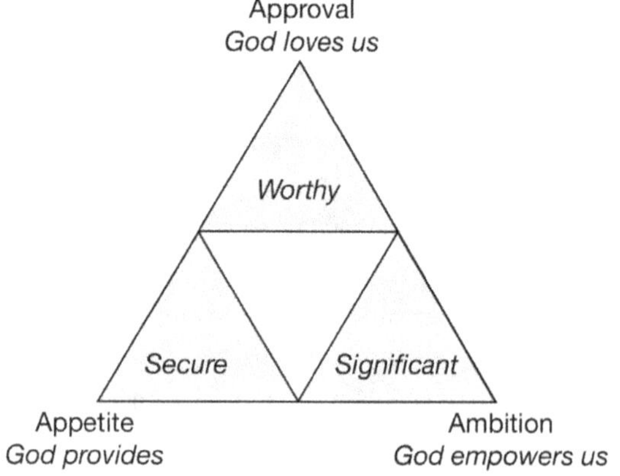

Colossians 1:9-12: "For this reason, since the day we heard about you, we have not stopped praying for you. We continually ask God to fill you with the knowledge of his will through all the wisdom and understanding that the Spirit gives, so that you may live a life worthy of the Lord and please him in every way: bearing fruit in every good work, growing in the knowledge of God, being strengthened with all power according to his glorious might so that you may have great endurance and patience, and giving joyful thanks to the Father, who has qualified you to share in the inheritance of his holy people in the kingdom of light."

Our calling: to be submitted followers of the King of Kings bringing His life, peace and righteousness to the world we live in.

CHAPTER 4

A DECISION-MAKING TOOL

You've probably heard of the story of the wise and foolish builders which Jesus told his followers:

"Therefore everyone who hears these words of mine and puts them into practice is like a wise man who built his house on the rock. The rain came down, the streams rose, and the winds blew and beat against that house; yet it did not fall, because it had its foundation on the rock. But everyone who hears these words of mine and does not put them into practice is like a foolish man who built his house on sand. The rain came down, the streams rose, and the winds blew and beat against that house, and it fell with a great crash." (Matthew 7:24-27)

The key is to learn to listen to what God is saying and to respond to that. Many people find it hard to recognize what God is saying in their lives. The Learning Circle[8] is a tool which helps us to listen to God and helps us make healthy decisions in our lives.

THE LEARNING CIRCLE EXPLAINED

It is based on Mark 1:14-15: "After John was put in prison, Jesus went into Galilee, proclaiming the good news of God. "The time has come," he said. "The kingdom of God is near. Repent and believe the good news!"

Time – two words in Greek:
Chronos and Kairos

Chronos

- The sequential passing of time; chronological time
- About dates and clock time

Kairos

- An event or moment or a crisis when time can seem to "stand still".
A period of "time" when chronos is of no importance.
- It could mark a significant shift in your life

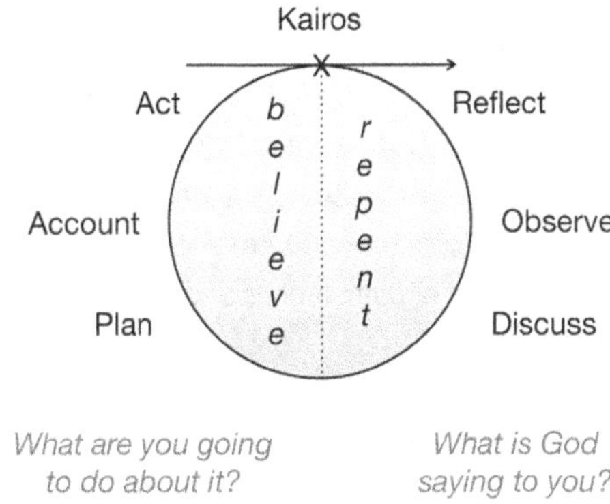

So a 'Kairos' time or moment can be an opportunity to look at a situation with the perspective of the Kingdom of God. A 'light bulb' moment, the penny drops or an 'Aha moment.' A 'kairos' moment can be big or small, positive or negative. Marriage, birth, someone dying. And you have the choice if you want to use a kairos moment or not.

Personal Examples:

BIG: move to Sheffield to learn more about discipleship we had to give up roles/jobs (pastor and counselor/ trainer) to become a trainee again.

SMALL: Normally on holidays we didn't plan anything because it's a holiday. But we noticed that time slips through our hands and we don't do things we both want to do. Or our neighbor who imitated our BBQ.
NEGATIVE: To find out that I'm (Jacolien) a do-er and my identity for a big part based was on what I'm doing or that I'm (Mark) still anxious about income although I believe in God's provision.

POSITIVE: God's provision in our live or to notice that

---

8   The Learning Circle is described by Mike Breen and Steve Cockram in *Building a Discipling Culture*

God is speaking to people and the desire to grow in listening to God.

Repent - in Greek: *metanoia*. This is the right side of the circle.

- A complete change of mind and heart ("be transformed by the renewing of your mind", Romans 12:2)
- A process of transformation that takes place within a person. Discipleship is a lifestyle of learning which begins with a change of heart.
- We need to start thinking differently about: God, who is a loving Father, ourselves, we are his sons and daughters, other people, they are created in God's image and circumstances and the world we live in.

We break down the repentance side of the circle into three steps:

- Observe: What's happened? Reactions, emotions. I.e. the holiday example: time slips away, disappointed, guilty
- Reflect: How did I feel? Why did this happen? Why did I react that way?
- Discuss: Bring other people into the process – if we want lasting change then we invite others into the process. For repentance to take hold we've got to share it with someone else, e.g. to share this in Huddle.

Notice that Observe and Reflect sometimes can merge into one.

After these three steps we ask the questions: What do you think God is saying to you? What is God's truth? What ungodly belief do you need to repent of?

We all know it is important to listen to God and be obedient. But there's another side as well. In Matthew 7:24 we read: "Therefore everyone who hears these words of mine and puts them into practice is like a wise man who built his house on the rock." That brings us to the left side of the circle.

Believe - In Greek: *pisteo*. This is what I am going to do about what God is saying to me.

- Active trust. A trust based on something you've been persuaded about; a continuing process of belief an action. Not only something internal but external (behavior)
- Can also be translated as faith; something you are sure about

We also break down the Believe side in 3 steps.

- Plan: what are you going to do? I.e. make a plan.
- Account: what are you accountable for and to whom? I.e. tell someone your plan.
- Act: go and do!

Questions:
What stood out for you in this Chapter?
Can you give an example of a recent kairos moment in your life? Was it big/small, positive/negative?
What is/was your tendency before you knew the Learning Circle when you processed things?

CHAPTER 5

INVITATION TO RELATIONSHIP AND CHALLENGE TO CHANGE

In this Chapter we'll have a look at two important principles, Invitation and Challenge. These two principles are found in Mark 1:16-20 where we can read: "As Jesus walked beside the Sea of Galilee, he saw Simon and his brother Andrew casting a net into the lake, for they were fishermen. 'Come, follow me,' Jesus said, 'and I will make you fishers of men.'" In this passage we often see only the challenge given by Jesus: "I'll make you fishers of men," but Jesus started with an invitation to come and follow.

INVITATION BY GOD THROUGH JESUS

Invitation is first of all that we as a disciple accept and receive the invitation of God to be with Him and enjoy his relationship with us. This is not about us doing our best which makes us acceptable, but accept that Jesus is our Saviour and that He wants to spend time with us. It is about abiding in Jesus.

"Live in me. Make your home in me just as I do in you. In the same way that a branch can't bear grapes by itself but only by being joined to the vine, you can't bear fruit unless you are joined with me. I am the Vine, you are the branches. When you're joined with me and I with you, the relation intimate and organic, the harvest is sure to be abundant. Separated, you can't produce a thing. (John 15: 4-5, MSG).

Here we read about an intimate and close relationship that we're invited into with Jesus. Being connected with Him is the source of everything we are.

INVITATION BY THE DISCIPLER

Second it is an invitation by the discipler. Jesus chose his disciples and invited them to follow him. He shared his life with them and they were part of his family. He started with covenant, being with them. He chose them, which was probably very encouraging. In that time it was more likely that disciples chose their teacher, but Jesus chose them!

"You did not choose me, but I chose you and appointed you so that you might go and bear fruit—fruit that will last—and so that whatever you ask in my name the Father will give you." (John 15:16)

Mike Breen summarises this well "Discipleship starts with an Invitation into relationship, just like Jesus did. He invited His disciples to follow and to stay with Him. There they have access to Jesus' life and all the safety, love and encouragement that reside there."[9]

As disciples we want to follow Jesus' lifestyle. In discipling other people it is important that we start by inviting them into our lives, to spend time with each other, to get to know each other, to encourage and love one another. Are we perfect like Jesus? No, but we're called to disciple others. We are all work in progress, but are called to follow Jesus and to ask him to help us!

---

9 Mike Breen, *Building a Discipling Culture*, p.18

Questions:

Who invites and challenges you? Is it in balance? And in what are you challenged? Kingdom responsibilities and/or Covenant relationship with God and others?

Discuss:

Are there people who like to hang around you? Are you aware of it? How can you become more conscious of being an example?

INTERNAL AND EXTERNAL CHANGE

To grow as a disciple we also need challenge. Only receiving invitation creates a cozy and comfortable atmosphere that could be nice for a while, but doesn't helps us to change.

Change is about challenge. C.S. Lewis said, "Every Christian is to become a little Christ."[10]

The goal of change is clear: we desire to grow to be more like Jesus in our character. This internal change will also affect how we will do things.

The first words of Jesus when He started his ministry were: "Repent, for the kingdom of heaven has come near." (Matthew 4:17 NIV)

The Greek word for repent is 'metanoia' which means a complete change or renewing of mind and heart. It is the same word used in Romans 12:2 where Paul wrote: "be transformed by the renewing of your mind".

It is a process of transformation that takes place within a person. What is it that needs to be changed?

- First of all our understanding of God. He is a loving Father.
- Secondly we need to understand who we are, His beloved sons and daughters.
- Thirdly we need to start looking at people like the Father does, with compassion and a longing to restore their relationships with Him. We need to look at situations with a kingdom perspective.

In this process of repentance, an internal change (change in our hearts, mindsets and character) will be followed by an external change (behavior and competence).

In the last few years it has become more important to us (Mark and Jacolien) to allow God to develop our character than to develop our skills. What we've learned is that character growth is much more important and lies at the foundation of everything. Disciples need to reflect Jesus' character and we need internal change for this.

---

10   C.S. Lewis, *Mere Christianity*, p177

A summary of Jesus character is in Galatians 5:22-23: "But the fruit of the Spirit is love, joy and peace, patience, kindness, goodness, faithfulness, gentleness and self-control."

It is striking that these are all characteristics rather than specific things we should do. It shows the importance of building our identity on who we are because of our family relationship with Jesus, not on the things we can achieve. This is the starting point for fruitfulness.

What Do We Know About Character Change?

One thing that's for sure: it takes time. Character change unfortunately does not happen over night. There is no point trying to rush it. We need to trust that God knows best when it's the right time. Character change requires us to deliberately involve God in our life every day. To take time apart to be quiet so that we can experience God's presence and listen to what He is saying to us.

Personal Example

For me (Jacolien) this means going out regularly for a walk by a local lake. During this walk, I watch and listen, I have a conversation with God, or sometimes I just enjoy being with Him. Hearing God brings me back to a place of rest so that I can focus on the right things.

To be in safe accountable relationships where we can receive challenge. When we look to Jesus we see that He starts by inviting the disciples to spend time with him, so that He could teach them and they had the opportunity to observe what He was doing to expand the Kingdom. Later in the gospels we read that He sends them out to proclaim that the Kingdom has come and heal the sick (Matthew 10, Luke 9, Luke 10). This is quite a challenge! In Luke 10:17 we read that the disciples returned, surprised and also encouraged!

An environment of only challenge can lead to stress because we live under a lot of pressure of others or maybe ourselves. That is the reason we need a culture where there is a balance between invitation and challenge. A culture of empowerment where we can grow.

Effective discipleship is based on a balance of:
- Invitation to relationship
- Challenge to change

Discuss:
How would an 'unbalanced' situation work out, i.e. too much emphasis on invitation or challenge?

Invitation and Challenge in a nutshell
Invitation = leader invites you in his personal life, in a way his comfort zone
Challenge = leader challenges you about some of your comfort zones

INTENTIONALITY

Fruitful discipleship is an intentional way of life. It is important to know what our challenge is when we disciple other people. Everyone has a natural tendency to invitation or challenge. When we're growing in discipling others it is important to know what is natural for us so that we know where we need to learn and grow.

This starts as a discipline. I (Mark) had to be very intentional about this and it didn't come naturally but in time it just became a welcome habit. Life would not feel right without it, it has become a lifestyle. The pathway to change starts with a discipline, which grows into habit and that becomes a lifestyle.

Personal Examples

Mark

Invitation: Rich and Anna Robinson (directors of 3DM Europe) invited us to be part of their extended family and to be part of the 3DM Europe team.

Challenges: I was a church leader and I had to become a learner/disciple again in a different (church) culture. This step was also a financial challenge, because we lost our steady income.

More recently: Living in a missional household is a challenge in the area's of control and (partly) giving up privacy.

Jacolien

Invitation by Sharon to live together in a missional household. We've started to build and grow our relationship (food, fun and prayers) We liked each other, there was chemistry. We started to do some mission together and found out that we had a shared missional calling.

Challenge: I had to give up personal comfort, space and rhythms and to have a healthy balance in having time on my own and together with Mark.

Questions (For a Disciple):

Where do you experience invitation and where challenge? And who is doing that?
If NOT: have you ever experienced it?
Where do you see God's invitation in your life? And where His challenge?

Questions (For a Discipler):

What is easier for you, to encourage people and make things comfortable for them and also to invite them into your life (Invitation)? Or to call people out of their comfort zone (Challenge)?
How can you invite people? What do you invite them into? Who can you invite?
Do you challenge people? If yes: how? If not: why not?
Do you know how you can challenge someone properly?

STEPPING STONE TWO

LIVING A BALANCED AND INTEGRATED LIFESTYLE

CHAPTER 6

BALANCED AND INTEGRATED RELATIONSHIPS

Missional Discipleship is All About Relationships.

When we look at Jesus' life we see three areas of relationships which are held in balance:
Relationship with the Father (UP)
Relationship with his community of disciples (IN)
Relationships with the world who didn't know him (OUT)

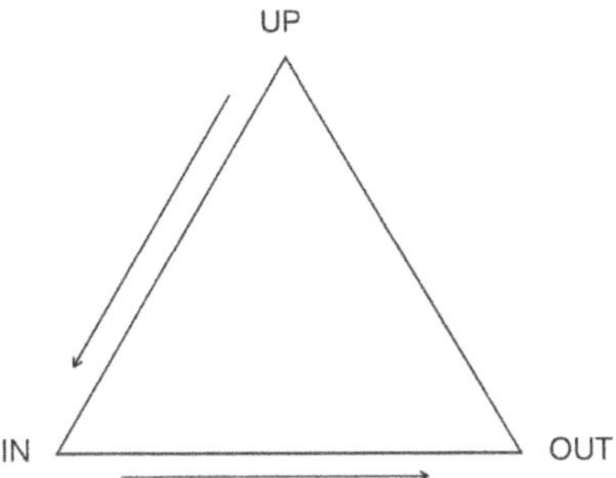

This UP-IN-OUT triangle helps us to reflect on the balance in our relationships and to be intentional about whom we spend time with, it is helpful in a busy life. In an integrated lifestyle the three areas of the triangle are part of our everyday life. Then there is no difference between sacred and secular anymore. Jesus brought his disciples with him on mission and they saw him also spending time with his Father.

FOUR IMPORTANT PRINCIPLES

As we look at the UP-IN-OUT relationships there are four important principles:
Balanced
Intentional
Integrated
Connected

Balanced
When we look at Jesus then we see He lived a balanced lifestyle. He lived out his life in three relationships: Covenant relationship with the Father (UP) and his disciples (IN) and Kingdom responsibilities towards the people who don't know Him (OUT). How did Jesus do this:

Read Together:
Luke 6: 12-19: "One of those days Jesus went out to a mountainside to pray, and spent the night praying to God. When morning came, he called his disciples to him and chose twelve of them, whom he also designated apostles: Simon (whom he named Peter), his brother Andrew, James, John, Philip, Bartholomew, Matthew, Thomas, James son of Alphaeus, Simon who was called the Zealot, Judas son of James, and Judas Iscariot, who became a traitor. He went down with them and stood on a level place. A large crowd of his disciples was there and a great number of people from all over Judea, from Jerusalem, and from the coastal region around Tyre and Sidon, who had come to hear him and to be healed of their diseases. Those troubled by impure spirits were cured, and the people all tried to touch him, because power was coming from him and healing them all."

Question:
*Can you identify the UP, IN and OUT relationships
in the passage?*

What Does This Mean For Us?
Our first and most important relationship is with our
Father in heaven.

UP - He is our source also for all our other relationships
in our lives. Jesus said that the first and greatest
commandment is: "Love the Lord your God with all your
heart and with all your soul and with all your mind."
(Matthew 22:27).

IN - This is about the relationship with family or
community. We see that Jesus first of all was focused
on calling his disciples and inviting them into his life and
discipling them. This are all the relationships we have
with people who are already following Jesus. These can
be people in our community, church etc.

"Therefore, as we have opportunity, let us do good to all
people, especially to those who belong to the family of

believers." (Galatians 6:10)

OUT - As soon as Jesus called his disciples they went
out to the world around them to build relationships
and to bless people. We are made to live together in
order to reach out to the world. To spend time and build
relationships with non-christians is very important!

It is not always easy to have a balance in relationships,
to divide our time equally between these three
relationships. Most of us and our churches/communities
are strong in maybe two of these areas.

UP and IN, focus on teaching and pastoring.
UP and OUT, loads of evangelistic activities, high
challenge. Not a very strong IN.
IN and OUT, strong relationships, incarnational ministry,
social engagement but a weak UP.

Intentional
We need to be intentional to invest in UP-IN-OUT
relationships, it won't happen automatically. It starts as
a discipline, then becomes a habit and eventually it will
be an integrated part of our lifestyle.

Integrated
UP-IN-OUT rhythms need to be part of every day life
in stead of an extra activity, like prayer meetings, social
meetings, evangelism activities. Our experience is that
life is easier and discipleship is more effective when it is
integrated in our lives.
Connected
It is important to see the UP-IN-OUT angles of the
triangle connected with one another and not as
separate areas.

UP-IN - to connect the UP and IN could mean that you
pray, listen to God and worship together in stead of
doing this on your own. In our household we've prayed
3 weekdays between 7:30 and 8:00am before we had
breakfast together.

IN-OUT - we do mission together. E.g. we visit people
who don't know Jesus yet in couples. But also this

means that if we find 'people of peace' (see Chapter 10) we bring them to our community so that our friends get to know them.

OUT-UP - we bring the supernatural in the OUT. E.g. by prayer and prophecy for and with people who don't know Jesus yet. We've prayed for neighbors, taxi drivers, a plumber, a physiotherapist, our landlord, people visiting our parties and one of the guys on a soccer field. Of course we've asked their permission for doing that.

Discuss:

How do you most easily connect with God?

Discuss:

How do you balance your time between your UP, IN and OUT relationships?

Are you doing UP and OUT with others in community? What are the areas of growth?

PREDICTABLE PATTERNS OR RHYTHMS

A simple way to integrate UP-IN-OUT in your life is to use predictable patterns or rhythms (see also Chapter 9). A rhythm is a pattern - something we're doing that is part of a our daily rhythm of life.

Why do you need rhythms? Understanding the principles of rhythms.
- Rhythms will help you to intentionally living a balanced and integrated lifestyle.
- Rhythms are linked with values
- Rhythms provide a framework of discipline, habit and lifestyle
- Rhythms create a pattern of life on life discipleship

We have daily rhythms for example for work, rest, prayer. Every day we individually take time to have quiet time with God. There are weekly rhythms also for work, rest and prayer. For example Mark and Jacolien are having time with God (praying, listening to God) as a couple every week. Also it is a rhythm to have a day of rest every week. There are monthly rhythms, for example a fun activity with the community. There are also annual rhythms like holidays and celebrations (birthday, Christmas, Easter). So for example, we're celebrating our birthdays with the people in our community.

A Few Comments About Rhythms
Rhythms aren't set for ever. They can be different and change from time to time: seasons, demographics.
You can have different rhythms or orbits for different (groups of) people.
Rhythms aren't supposed to be written in stone, make sure there is space for spontaneity or move of the Holy Spirit when He asks to do something unexpected.
Proximity is key for rhythms, but when you can't meet face-to-face think about the use of technology. We use WhatsApp, Skype and Zoom when we aren't able to meet due to distance.

Questions:
What stood out to you in this Chapter?
Balance: Score yourself around the Triangle for UP/ IN/OUT: 1 = low and 10 = high.
Integrated: Score yourself how integrated the triangle is in your life?
Connected: Score how connected are the different areas in your life?
Where are there opportunities to develop? What is already an established rhythm or pattern?

CHAPTER 7

UP

The evening before Jesus died He told his disciples to remain in Him, the vine.

"Live in me. Make your home in me just as I do in you" and "When you're joined with me and I with you, the relation intimate and organic, the harvest is sure to be abundant." (John 15:5 MSG)

This is one of the last messages from Jesus to his disciples. Fruitfulness in our lives always starts with having that intimate relationship. Fruit is what we can see but this organic relationship is something that is not very visible. This is about attitude, being (rather before than doing).

We call this the UP. The grace is always flowing from the UP in our lives. It is not about us making and striving for fruit in our lives but a natural, organic outcome of this amazing love in us. His love is the engine. He is more than enough.

"I am the true vine, and my Father is the gardener. He cuts off every branch in me that bears no fruit, while every branch that does bear fruit he prunes so that it will be even more fruitful. You are already clean because of the word I have spoken to you. Remain in me, as I also remain in you. No branch can bear fruit by itself; it must remain in the vine. Neither can you bear fruit unless you remain in me. "I am the vine; you are the branches. If you remain in me and I in you, you will bear much fruit; apart from me you can do nothing. If you do not remain in me, you are like a branch that is thrown away and withers; such branches are picked up, thrown into the fire and burned. If you remain in me and my words remain in you, ask whatever you wish, and it will be done for you. This is to my Father's glory, that you bear much fruit, showing yourselves to be my disciples. (John 15: 1-8)

'Remain in the vine' - seven times in this short passage! Jesus had an ongoing relationship with his Father and made time to pray and to listen to Him. We read regularly in the gospels that he went away on his own or with his disciples to pray.

For example in Luke 5:16: "But Jesus often withdrew to lonely places and prayed." So as followers of Jesus we also need to prioritize our relationship with God in our lives and make sure we have time to 'abide'.

What does that look like in our lives?

INDIVIDUALLY

First of all there is that personal relationship of us with God. Similar to Jesus who went up the mountain on his own to be with the Father.

Question:
What are the ways you connect with God?

We'll take a look at prayer, Bible reading and worship. By the way, there are more ways to connect with God. Liz, a good friend of ours, connects with God while listening to music (of all styles) or during cooking!

Prayer

Prayer is communication with God. It is part of relationship. To share your life, thoughts, feelings with Him. Psalm 62 is a great example how God is our rock and refuge and how to do this. "Pour out your heart to him, for God is our refuge" (Psalm 62:8).

How to Start With This?

Having the right attitude and focusing our hearts on God. The Lords prayer starts with: "Our Father who is in Heaven, hallowed be your name" (Matthew 6:9). It starts to address God for who he is - his character.

Psalm 100 says: "Know that the Lord is God. It is he who made us, and we are his; we are his people, the sheep of his pasture. Enter his gates with thanksgiving and his courts with praise; give thanks to him and praise his name. For the Lord is good and his love endures forever; his faithfulness continues through all generations." (Psalm 100: 3-5).
Verse 4 in other translations: 'Enter with the password: "Thank you!" (MSG) and 'Be thankful and say so to ho Him' (AMP).

And another verse says: "Rejoice always, pray continually, give thanks in all circumstances; for this is God's will for you in Christ Jesus." (1 Thessalonians 5:16). The discipline of thanksgiving is very powerful and helps us to look beyond ourselves and our circumstances. Although circumstances are sometimes very hard, there is always something to be thankful for. It is not about giving thanks for difficult circumstances, but to keep being thankful in all circumstances.

Jacolien - when praying I usually start with a few minutes to thank God before starting to pray for my 'daily bread'. Listening to worship music helps me to bring myself in a place of praise and thanksgiving.

Questions:
Do you feel you can live in an attitude of thanksgiving for God's goodness? If not, what are the barriers?
How can you grow a discipline of thanksgiving in your life?

Praying is also asking. Jesus says in the parable about the persistent widow that we should asking and not give up (Luke 18:1-8)! This is an encouragement and challenge to pray and ask for the things we need and for the people and world around us.

Prayer is not only us talking, but also listening to God. Sheep hear and recognize the voice of the shepherd. Jesus describes himself as the Good Shepherd. "My sheep listen to my voice; I know them, and they follow me." (John 10:27)

God is still speaking in the here and now and He wants that intimate relationship with us. Jesus went regularly on the mountain on his own to pray and to listen to His Father.

Personal Example:

I (Jacolien) have grown in the last few years to stop and listen. It is not always easy to be still and make space in our lives to listen. It starts with discipline and bringing ourselves in place with no distraction and also to find a way where it is easy for us to connect with God. Some examples include being on your own in a room and being still and reflecting, writing down your thoughts about God, listening to worship music, reading the Bible and listening for what God is saying, or going out into nature.

Question:

Do you have other examples of how you're listening to God?

my own life and for people i'm feeling prompted to pray for. This is more focused and asking God to bring his Kingdom in my world and the world around me. What has started as a discipline, became a habit and is now a lifestyle. Learning to stop and listen carefully. To focus on God and ask what He says. When I lived in England, this meant walking around Damflask reservoir once a week and during this time asking Him questions and also paying attention to the nature around me if He spoke through this. So often He has spoken through his gentle voice in my mind. A word of encouragement or guidance. "Be still and know that I am God" (Psalm 46:10) is an important encouragement for me to become silent and give opportunity to God to speak to me. Then to write this down and be grateful to have a relationship with a living and speaking God.

Questions:

Do you know a way you can bring yourself into a place of stillness? Discuss 'stillness.'
What is your rhythm for personal prayer?
What do you need to start as a discipline, which will become a habit and then a lifestyle?

Personal Example:

I (Jacolien) try to go at least once a week to go out for a walk and during that time I'm listening and praying to God. When I'm walking I'm starting to focus on God and who He is and start with listening what He is saying to me as his daughter during the first half of that walk. Then after that I start to pray about circumstances in

Bible Reading

To read the word of God is very important so that we build our faith and stand on the truth. To renew our minds so that we learn to think God's truth instead of getting caught up in our own (ungodly) thoughts and beliefs. "Do not conform to the pattern of this world, but be transformed by the renewing of your mind. Then you will be able to test and approve what God's will is—his good, pleasing and perfect will." (Romans 12:2). When we're hearing God then He never speaks against the word in the Bible. So having knowledge of the Bible helps us to hear and to discern what God is saying.

We also have the word to protect ourselves and fight the spiritual battle we're all involved in. "Take the helmet of salvation and the sword of the Spirit, which is the word of God." (Ephesians 6:17). When we know what is written in the Bible we can stand against the devil, like when Jesus was tempted by the devil in the desert (Luke 4)

We've also received the Bible to encourage one another. "Therefore encourage one another with these words." (1 Thessalonians 4:18)

Worship

Worship is not only singing songs. It is important that we not only worship God by singing a song but with our whole life. "Therefore, I urge you, brothers and sisters, in view of God's mercy, to offer your bodies as a living sacrifice, holy and pleasing to God—this is your true and proper worship." (Romans 12:1)

Of course we can praise God with music, but also in arts and all kinds of creativity. God is the ultimate source of creativity. To express God's character in arts can be a great way to express our relationship with the Father. There is no one right way to worship, as long as we have the right attitude in our hearts. That it is not about me and my gifts, it is about the great Giver of gifts.

Question:

How do you worship God in your daily life?

Discuss

This is an important topic! Try to get lots of examples - especially from your own life.
When you are in a group get everyone to try each other's examples - have fun!

TOGETHER WITH OTHERS

Why do we pray and worship together? In Matthew 18:19-20 we read: "Again, truly I tell you that if two of you on earth agree about anything they ask for, it will be done for them by my Father in heaven. For where two or three gather in my name, there am I with them." Here Jesus is talking about a shared prayer request and that when we gather in His name He will be with us. In His name we are gathered and in His name we pray.

In Acts we read about the first followers of Jesus: "They devoted themselves to the apostles' teaching and to fellowship, to the breaking of bread and to prayer." (Acts 2:42)

"Every day they continued to meet together in the tempel courts. They broke bread in their homes and ate together with glad and sincere hearts, praising God and enjoying the favor of all the people." (Acts 2:46-47)

- It reflects that we are one body.
- It bring us closer to God and closer to each other, unity.
- Helps us to be vulnerable with each other, purity.
- It is spiritual warfare standing strong with each other.
- Pray for one another, so we can help each other.
- Good for 'OUT'. The more we pray, the more miracles we'll see.
- Grace flows from UP > IN > OUT.
- Bringing the fivefold together and our different gifting.
- Learning to hear God in different ways.
- It can be energetic and fun.

There can be a difference in how people do experience praying and worshipping together and may be more or less confident in doing this. Extraverted people might be energised and introverted might be challenged by praying and worshiping together in a (small) group. This is ok and good to recognize these differences so that we can learn and celebrate these.

Our experience is that praying and listening to God in a group is encouraging and stimulating. In our household we prayed 3 times a week between 7:30-8:00am and we always started with thanksgiving (UP) followed by sharing our prayer points, praying for one another and other people who needed prayer (IN). We also prayed together for not-yet Christians we knew (OUT). We had some friends who also wanted to come and joined our morning prayers once a week. When someone in our house was away and wanted to join in, then they participated via internet (like Face time, Zoom etc) so that we could hear and see each other!

It is important to find a time suitable for you. Although no one in our household played an instrument we still did (musical) worship together. We used a playlist with worships songs and we just listened to this and sang along with some great worship leaders!

If we can pray and worship together in the household, we can learn to pray and worship basically anywhere.

Examples of How You Can Worship Together:
- Being thankful together
- Rhythms of prayer
- Worship & Word
- Retreat together
- Fast together
- Giving together

Questions:
With whom could you pray together regularly?
What might this look like?
Where are opportunities for prayer with people you are in community with or folks you do OUT with?
(integration of UP with IN and OUT)

CHAPTER 8

HEARING GOD AND PROPHECY

In the previous chapters we have spoken several times about 'hearing God' and how we can listen for ourselves, as a community for each other and even for non-Christians. The question 'What does God say?' is an important question for growing as a follower of Jesus. We realize that this question is not easy for everyone to answer. That is also the reason why we want to go deeper into this. Since hearing God and prophecy are connected with one another we will discuss both parts.

WHAT DOES THE BIBLE SAY?

When we look in the Bible we discover that God is not an impersonal God, but that He speaks to people. The Bible is full of stories about how God's children experience His guidance and follow His voice. We were created to understand God's voice, it is, as it were, in our DNA.

The Old Testament

This started in the paradise where Adam and Eve walked with God and it was very natural for them to communicate with him. Even after the Fall, we see that God is looking for man and asks: "Where are you?". Later we see that God spoke to Noah and Abraham and to Joseph through dreams. And again later we read that God speaks to his people through leaders and prophets and that there was a great responsibility for them to follow his voice. "Call upon me, and I will answer you, I will make you known great, wonderful things, things that are completely unknown to you." (Jeremiah 33: 3) Also in the Psalms regularly comes the incentive to go to God with everything that keeps us busy and to trust that He will answer.

The New Testament

The New Testament is then full of examples of how God speaks to his disciples and how they learn to understand and follow his voice. It begins with Jesus calling his disciples. He literally invites them and to follow his voice. Jesus says in John 10:14 "I am the good shepherd. I know my sheep and my sheep know me". Then in verse 27 even more specifically "My sheep listen to my voice, I know them and they follow me." There is not 'my prophet', or 'pastors' hear my voice. No, it says 'my sheep'. So this is not about special 'anointed' people but 'ordinary' followers of Jesus. They can listen to his voice. It is a promise and at the same time an encouragement from Jesus that hearing his voice for his followers is self-evident!

In addition to listening to God's voice for our relationship with him, we can also hear his voice for others. Here too the New Testament is clear about:
"I will pour out My Spirit on all people... and they will prophesy." (Acts 2:14-18)
"... eagerly desire spiritual gifts, especially the gift of prophecy." (1 Corinthians 14:1)
"For you can all prophesy in turn so that everyone may be instructed and encouraged." (1 Corinthians 14:31)

In Acts we read that the Holy Spirit is poured out on his disciples and then on everyone who believes, both Jews and gentiles. The whole book of Acts is full of stories about how God speaks to his disciples in various ways and guides them in their lives, traveling and preaching the gospel. Peter even sees a vision through which he is going to tell the gospel to non-Jews (Acts 10:9-23). The first Christians live in dependence on hearing his voice and guidance (Acts 13:2) and Paul is guided by the Holy Spirit (Acts 16: 6-10).

Through the Holy Spirit we can understand God's voice and guidance. In the Old Testament, the Holy Spirit worked only temporarily, in special situations, by people who had been specially chosen for this, such as his prophets. In the New Testament we see that the Spirit is poured out on all believers!

"If you love me, keep my commands. And I will ask the Father, and he will give you the spirit of truth. The world can not accept him, because it neither sees him nor knows him. But you know him, for he lives with you and will be in you." (John 14:15-17)

Jesus tells what the Holy Spirit is doing: "But when he, the Spirit of truth, comes, he will guide you into the truth. He will not speak on his own; he will speak only what he hears, and he'll tell you what is yet to come. He will glorify me because it is from me that he will know what he will make known to you. All that belongs to the Father is mine. That is why I said the Spirit will receive from me what will make known to you." (John 16: 13-15)
"No eye has seen, no ear has heard … but God has shown it to us by His Spirit ". (1 Corinthians 2:16)

By being aware of the presence of the Holy Spirit, being filled by him, will connect us with the voice of the Father.

TUNING IN TO GOD

Listening to God is actually like tuning to the right wavelength with a radio. The radio waves are constantly around us, but we have to fine-tune the radio to receive it. You can also compare it to a wifi network. There are countless wifi networks in the air but to make contact you have to select the right network and whether or not to enter a password. The starting point is that God speaks, that is not the problem. The point is that we attune to Him, to select the right wavelength or wifi network.

Our friend Cath Livesey gives the following practical steps[1] that can help us to understand God's voice:

- Align your thinking with the truth that God is still speaking today, also to you and me.
- Know who you are. Start with knowing who God is and who you are (Identity). God is our heavenly Father who loves us and wants to communicate with us. We are his beloved sons and daughters. Do we really know who we are? We hear God's voice not by

works, not by striving, but because we know him as Father and that He loves us. Hearing God is about who you are not what you do. It is not something we achieve through hard work or 'super spirituality'. "For you did not receive a spirit that makes you a slave again to fear, but you received the Spirit of sonship. And by him we cry " Abba, Father."' (Romans 8:15)
- Believe that you will hear God's voice. God gives promises in the Bible (see above) that we as children can hear and understand his voice. Growing in this is about believing in this and with these promises to broaden and renew our thinking.
- Recognize all the 'normal' everyday ways God does speak to us and be thankful. God usually speaks through the 'ordinary', although we may want it to happen through special and special things (burning bush, an angel of the Lord, a beautiful vision). An important part of learning to tune in to his voice is to recognize this. We are not always so good at recognising this. We are disciples who lead normal lives. It is important that we integrate God into our ordinary, daily life. Some of these normal and everyday ways how God speaks to us are:
- through our conscience
- by experiencing a sense of peace
- due to circumstances and events
- by other people
- by nature
- Understand that we all understand God in different ways. We are all different people and have different personalities. The Bible does not describe one particular way how people have understood God's voice. They were all different experiences. God often connects with who we are as a person. Our challenge is to find out what suits us. How do we put ourselves in a position where it is 'easier' for us to focus on God.? For someone who has a preference for introversion, this can mean that becoming quiet literally means sitting quietly and meditatively praying and listening. For someone who is extrovert this probably does not work as well because he/she is distracted. Such a person can

---

1 C. Livesey, *My Sheep Have Ears*, p.18-24

often better concentrate on God during a walk or an activity, even during ironing! The temptation may be to compare yourself with a well known person with a Christian or prophetic ministry, but that person is different and probably also experiences God differently. Do not compare yourself so much with others, but look for the way you can become silent and focus on God.

If you doubt if it was God's voice remind yourself that often the things God shares are spontaneous, of special quality, resonating and life giving.

Question:
How does God speak to you?

BARRIERS TO HEARING GOD'S VOICE

It is also important to become aware of barriers that can prevent us from hearing God's voice. By this we mean specific and personal thought patterns or emotions.

Cath Livesey says that these 'other voices' can function as a blockade, so that we create a barrier between God or as a filter through which God's voice is distorted. The intention is that we learn to explain these voices.

Personal Example:
Brought up in a very traditional church culture I (Mark) wasn't familiar with hearing God. When I got older and started to visit conferences and started to step out in faith I learned more and more about the gifts of the Holy Spirit, hearing God and prophecy. I learned a lot during the time we lived abroad, in the Caribbean, where we helped to set up a Christian rehabilitation center for drug addicts, and back in the Netherlands during the Alpha ministry training. But to be honest I had difficulties with hearing God.

Reflecting on it with the knowledge I now have, I think I was unconscious of some barriers to hear God's voice. To mention some of them: for a long time I believed that God only speaks to special gifted people and because I didn't receive that special gift God didn't speak to me. Later, when I tried to hear God's voice, I rationalized that it was just my own thoughts or I started to doubt it was the right thing to share with people.

Examples of other voices that can form a barrier are:
- Disbelief: Usually the belief that "God never speaks to me'" or "I can not hear God". They could have told us, or we've told them and started to believe them.
- Rationalism: this barrier exists when we lean too much on our own understanding and worldly wisdom. It is not wrong to rationalise, but over-emphasis will hinder us hearing God.
- Fear: Fears are based on lies and they stop drawing us close to God. E.g. fear that God will say something that is scary to me, fear of getting it wrong, fear of deception - frightened that the enemy is going to speak to us rather than God, fear of intimacy - because of our own brokenness we fear that intimacy that is associated with hearing the Father's voice.

Personal Example:

I (Jacolien) regularly worried that I was wrong when I thought that God was saying something. This prevented me from saying something specific about what I thought or what God was doing during a conversation or prayer. I was more concerned with myself, how I would look, rather than obeying God and blessing others. This has changed fortunately. I am now free of these thoughts so that I can be a more effective channel of God's love.

- Shame: Shame has the effect of completely dampening and distorting the voice of God. It allows us to withdraw from God's presence out of a feeling of unworthiness.
- Our agendas: These often function more as a filter than a blockade. To be honest, this is a 'voice' that is often somewhat more difficult to expose and can even look like working in God's kingdom. These subtle filters can be: our opinions, our plan for other people, our desire to impress people, trying to meet their needs, or our theology.

Question:

Which barriers to hearing God and sharing with others do you recognize?

How to Deal With Barriers

There are a few steps you can take to deal with barriers:

- Recognize the block. We can pray that God shows us what is in our way to hear him.
- Forgiveness is sometimes the next step. To forgive other people who have bothered us to hear God or ourselves if we have this blockade.
- Repent and believe (think of this biblical process from Mark 1:15). Choose to no longer agree with the 'other voice' - a blockage or barrier. Do not feed these thoughts.
- Repent is changing our thinking (metanoia). Choose to take hold of the truth and embrace a new mindset: "I'm a deeply loved child of God. My identity is found in knowing God as Father. I hear Him because He's my Dad. I hear Him because He loves me and wants to speak to me. I do not have to strive to hear His voice ... "
- Believe is also to act according to this truth. To align life in the opposite direction of our blockade and our behavior with our internal change (change of thinking).

Personal Example:

I (Jacolien) found it hard to imagine something when listening to God. The fact that I would say that God says something to me or someone, I found a big step. My experience influenced how comfortable I felt about it. God speaks, but especially through the Bible, was my starting point. I still believe in this, but God speaks in so many ways, through nature (see also psalm 8) by others and events. The question, of course, is how to interpret or translate what we hear and how we keep a healthy image of God that is in line with the Bible and what we believe from God.

PROPHECY

We read about prophecy both in the Old and New Testament. The Hebrew word for prophecy is derived from a word which means 'to bubble forth, as from a fountain'.[2]

---

2 https://www.biblestudytools.com/dictionary/prophet/

In Greek, prophecy means 'to pronounce' or 'to speak for someone else'. In prophecy we often think of receiving information about the future. Although this can certainly be the case, this is not the only one. Prophecy also relates to the passing on of God's truth. We therefore describe prophecy as:

- Fore-telling - speaking about the future - God tells us what is yet to come (for example the famine in Acts 11:27-28)
- Forth-telling— speaking about the present - communicating God's heart for the present (think of the prophet Nathan when he talks to David about his affair with Bathsheba). This can relate to: Listening to and understanding the heart of God.
- To proclaim the heart of God / to communicate the heart of God.
- Proclamation of God's potential about a person's life.

Skepticism

When we talk about prophecy, it may be that we feel uncomfortable. This may be because it is an unknown territory, but also because of stories of abuses with prophecy. What has helped me (Mark) are Mike Bickle's comments about wrong assumptions we can have. He mentions the following three:

- Character equals anointing.
- Anointing equals divine endorsement of ministry style.
- Anointing equals 100 percent doctrinal accuracy.

God chooses to work through imperfect people, including you and me. We should not automatically consider the spiritual gifts in one's ministry as invalid because of his or her shortcomings, the fact that the person has a different 'style of ministry' or that in some areas we have a theological difference. Again, we see the importance of discipleship and character development as part of it.

A FRAMEWORK

A good framework to use for hearing God and prophecy is the Triangle UP, IN and OUT. We can hear God's voice for ourselves (UP), for our brothers and sisters (IN) and for non-believers (OUT).

The UP Dimension

Hearing God and prophecy always starts with the UP, our relationship with God. The tendency could be to focus on the Kingdom aspect. It's important that we hear God's voice for ourself - in a way that will deepen our relationship with our heavenly Father. When we do not only pray to God, but also start to listen then we change a monologue in a dialogue and this will change our prayer life forever.

The IN Dimension

An important aspect is listening to God's voice for others. This is also where we clearly see the meaning of the word 'prophecy' (for someone else speaking). A simple definition is: hearing God speak and repeating what He says.

It is not about how spectacular our words/prophecies are but about connecting people with God's Father heart for them. In the Bible we read that the gift of prophecy is not only for special people. Paul says in 1 Corinthians 14:1 "Follow the way of love and eagerly desire spiritual gifts, especially the gift of prophecy."

We can all stretch out to understand God's voice for others and that is very nice to build each other with. Paul also gives a guideline that is very helpful: "But everyone who prophecies speaks to men for their strengthening, encouragement and comfort... he who prophecies edifies the church." (1 Corinthians 14:3-4).

Personal Example:

We regularly listen for each other in our community. For example at a birthday. We put the birthday boy or girl in the middle and are silent and listening to God for 3 minutes. Then tell what we've heard. The challenge is to only share what we have actually heard or seen and not immediately give it a meaning if we don't know. It is then up to the person to pray about what a word or image means. It is cool to encourage each other! Of course it can also happen spontaneously. The idea is that you have to pray for someone and ask God for an encouragement for that person and then share it. This does not always have to be in person, but can also be done through email.

Also I (Jacolien) listened to God during Lent a few times a week for people I know and emailed these words of encouragement to them. It was great to train myself in listening to God for others and hearing their responses.

What is the connection between prophecy and discipleship? Cath Livesey says that prophecy resources discipleship.

Through the gift of prophecy, we are growing closer to God's Father's heart and are also being equipped to step out into His Kingdom. By continuing to listen to God and to take decisions in line with this, we continue to grow as a follower of Jesus. In difficult times it helps us to hold on to what God has said.

The learning circle (Chapter 4) helps us to ask the question: "What does God say?" and to process that. It is important to complete the whole circle. There may be a tendency to move from the Kairos, in this case what we think God said, to observe and reflect without doing anything else with it. The 'discuss' step in the circle indicates that we share with others what we have heard of God. They can ask questions and help to interpret and apply it. Sharing can sometimes be difficult, but this is very important. Involving others also prevent us from going directly from the Kairos to 'act'.

We need each other when it comes to interpreting and applying what we have heard from God.

Some Important Things:

To hear God and share something for someone else can be scary. The main thing is willing to be available so that God can use you. You'll grow by stepping out.
Operate in a culture of love, humility and service. It's all about serving and being humble.
We need guidelines, boundaries and spiritual maturity.

The OUT Dimension

Prophecy empowers mission. I can take the love of God out into the world. A listening lifestyle is going to enable us to do OUT more effectively.

Personal Example:

Prophecy started to make more sense to me (Mark) when I heard a testimony of someone who used listing to God and prophecy in mission. She used it to reach out to non believers. Not only with words, but also with what she called 'prophetic acts'. Which basically means that you live out God's truth. For me that resonated a lot and suddenly the whole prophetic made more sense. From that point I was eager to learn more. I attended the Prophecy Course where we got teaching input, practical advise how to deal with ungodly beliefs, but also the opportunity to practice. In our household we've started to practice it as well. I'm still learning, but I'm growing in hearing God's voice and sharing prophetic words and pictures with others.

Listening to God begins by asking him where the people are where we can go. Which hearts has He prepared? Where is the harvest field? Ask if God touches our hearts so that we are moved for those who do not yet know God. Looking at the people around us with spiritual eyes.

We have a great gift for the world. First of all, we can prophesy about non-Christians. As long as we handle this carefully and follow the guidelines with our language and approach, and assuring us that what we say is encouraging, comforting and constructive. It is important that we create a safe environment, such as women approaching women and men approaching men.

Personal Example:

During Halloween, we, as a community, gave encouraging words to the children and parents who came to our house. We had prepared this carefully by asking God in advance to give us words and then writing them on beautiful cards. We also made sure that we had nice sweets in the house which the children were the first to receive. Then we asked the children, with their parents, whether they also wanted to receive a 'heavenly blessing'. Everyone said "yes" and then they could pick a card and read what was on it. Everyone reacted positively and the parents often also wanted to draw a card. It opened conversations about God and we could even pray with a number of people.

Prophecy also gives vision and direction. We need vision and listening to God for this is important. (Proverbs 29:18). We can all have good ideas and for the explorers among us it is not that difficult, but what is a 'God' idea? What does God call us? When listening to God it is about asking the Spirit what He is doing and where we may cooperate with him.

This is similar when we start a missional community. One of the first steps is to find God and listen to him for a missional vision. As leaders of a community it is important that we set aside time to listen to God for wisdom and direction. Examples are: a month of prayer and fasting, a week where prayer and worship are central, setting up a prayer room where you can pray 24/7 for the community and listening to God.

A listening lifestyle is the daily prayer "Lord, where do you bring me today and with whom do you want me to talk about your Kingdom?"

Exercise
To practice prophecy use these activations.

Activation 1
Start in a place of thanksgiving and praise. Psalm 100 tells us that we enter into the Lord's presence through thanksgiving and praise. So spend some time giving thanks for all the blessings God has poured into your life and then engage in praising Him for who He is.
Rest in the Fathers love. Remind yourself of your covenant identity as his beloved child. Enjoy being still in his presence, receiving his peace and knowing that the Father delights to speak to you.

Fix your thoughts on Jesus. Meditate a while on some of his names (light of the world, saviour, bread of life etc).

Contemplate the visual descriptions we have of him in scriptures. Allow worship of Jesus to fill your heart and delight in him.

Welcome the presence of the Holy Spirit. Spend some time honoring him as the Spirit of Truth. Lay down your agendas before him and surrender to his leading.
Ask him to speak. Remember that God speaks in many different ways. So you may find that a fleeting image pops into your head, or the name of a friend, or a verse for the Bible. It may be something s simple as a sense of peace or love. Just go with it: don't dismiss it. Write it down and give thanks.

Activation 2
Ask God for a Bible character to share to another person in the group, which somehow represent him/her. Also ask God why this Bible character?

Activation 3
Imagine Jesus in front of you - what is He saying or doing?

Activation 4
Ask God for an encouraging Bible verse or passage. It doesn't matter what it is, as long as it is encouraging! If you are really stuck just pick a favourite verse.
After that we ask the Holy Spirit who to give it to. Who does God want to encourage with this verse or passage? Then we are going to share the verse or passage with that person.
This exercise works really well in a big group setting. In a small group it's likely that some people won't be given a verse/passage. It's important to emphasise that the objective is that we all step out in listening to God, not that everyone is given a verse/passage.

Books and Resources:
My Sheep Have Ears by Cath Livesey. She also has developed 'The Prophecy Course', which you can find at www.accessibleprophecy.com.
Can You Hear Me? Tuning In to the God Who Speaks by Brad Jersak.
Growing in the Prophetic by Mike Bickle.

CHAPTER 9

IN

When Jesus started his ministry one of the first things He did was to call his disciples.

Question:
Why do you think Jesus called his disciples?

"Jesus went up on a mountainside and called to him those he wanted, and they came to him. He appointed twelve that they might be with him and that he might send them out to preach and to have authority to drive out demons." (Mark 3:13-15)

Jesus could do his ministry on his own. No doubt about that. But He choose these disciples to be with him and to work with him.

LOVE ONE ANOTHER

Mark: My focus is often on the things Jesus and his disciples did and the commandment He gave to go and make disciples. My attention is certainly not on the fact that they hang out together. But if we read through the gospels we find out that Jesus gave his disciples another commandment as well.
"Love one another. As I have loved you, so you must love one another. By this everyone will know that you are my disciples, if you love one another." (John 13: 34-35)

There are three things that stood out for me in this verse about loving one another.
The first one is 'As I have loved you'. The way Jesus loved his disciples is what we call sacrificial love. He laid down his life, literally, for his disciples and served them.
The second is that He commands his disciples to become like Jesus. Love one another as I did. This is what we call transformational love. The disciples will become more and more like Jesus. By the way it's good to be aware that this is a process. In the Bible you don't see a quick fix. Growing in character is always a process.
The third is visible love. The way they get along with one another will be noticed by people around them.

In Acts 2:42-47 we see the first expression of Jesus' new commandment. "They devoted themselves to the apostles' teaching and to fellowship, to the breaking of bread and to prayer. Everyone was filled with awe at the many wonders and signs performed by the apostles. All the believers were together and had everything in common. They sold property and possessions to give to anyone who had need. Every day they continued to meet together in the temple courts. They broke bread in their homes and ate together with glad and sincere hearts, praising God and enjoying the favor of all the people. And the Lord added to their number daily those who were being saved."

The principles of 'IN' from Acts 2:
Being devoted - give time and resources.

Willing to learn.
Fellowship.
Lord's supper.
Pray and worship together.
Expecting wonders - praying for healing and miracles.
Sharing resources.
Being generous.
Eat together.
Meetings in temple and homes.

ACTS 2 PRINCIPLES NOW AND BEYOND

The main question of course is how can we do this now? One thing that's sure is that we can't go back to Acts. It was a different time, country and culture. But what we can do is to look at these principles and see how we can apply them.

In order to use the principles we need to change our mindset, to start to think differently. In our culture we are 'programmed' to be individualistic and as self sufficient as possible. We are not used to living as community. Something I discovered in my life is that I separated my work, my church life and my private life - even when I was a pastor. For example I was hesitating to build friendships with people in the church where I was working. But when we look at Jesus then He called his disciples or co-workers my friends.

In Christian culture we usually expect people to behave or believe before they belong. But to experience authentic community, people need to know they are accepted - that they belong first.
A healthy community can lead them to belief in Jesus and in time to changed behavior patterns.

FIVE USEFUL AREAS

Here are five useful areas which helped us to organize the principles of Acts 2:

- Predictable Patterns
- Sustainable Patterns
- Structured and Spontaneous
- Sacred and Secular
- Purpose and Play

Predictable Patterns

This is a simple way to integrate UP-IN-OUT in your life. Why do you need these patterns or rhythms? They will help you to be intentional and to live a balanced and integrated lifestyle. Especially in our busy lives it's helpful to have specific rhythms so that everybody can plan around it. To make it more concrete:
Food - we all need 2-3 meals a day, so why not invite people to join you? Do you eat together as a family?
Fun - doing fun things together will help you to create community.
Fellowship - Fellowship is from the Greek word 'koinonia'. The root of the word fellowship means "to hold something in common." From the usage of the word, we can conclude that fellowship is a word that describes a relationship that is dependent on more than one individual. It is an interdependent relationship. 'Koinonia' is used nineteen times in the New Testament and in addition to being translated as fellowship it is also translated by the words, contribution, sharing and participation. This word shows that action is always included in its meaning. Fellowship, is not just being together, it is doing together!
Worship and prayers - great opportunity to combine UP and IN.

Sustainable Patterns

Make sure that the patterns or rhythms you choose are sustainable. They don't have to sustain for eternity, but at least for a while. Choose the right rhythms for the season. Seasons can be within a year (summer, winter) or in life (season as a student or season with young children). In which season are you and your family in? To make the rhythms easier to adopt in everyday life think about these two important aspects:
Integration - If patterns are integrated in your ordinary life it will be easier then doing a lot of extra activities.
Delegation - Involving others lightens the load of what you need to do. Start as soon as possible to involve people in what you do, that makes it less demanding for you and helps others to take responsibility and become more engaged.

Structured and Spontaneous

Structure and planning is necessary when you have to deal with a group of people of any size. With busy lives you can't always organize something at the last moment. Don't forget to do spontaneous things as well. Sometimes you need to set a date (structure) to do something spontaneous. Make the spontaneous things simple, ask yourself whom you can invite during simple things you already doing (watching movies, sports, shopping, walk, etc.) Some important topics to think of are:

Rest

When there is a planning people can make sure that they are rested and therefore be present when they need to be present.

Sacred and Secular

Often people divide their lives into sacred and secular. Everything we do in church is sacred and outside it is secular. Leading a church or ministry is sacred while other jobs are secular. Therefore when they are together as Christians they feel the need to do 'spiritual activities.' We don't believe in sacred and secular. We believe that every part of our lives is sacred, including enjoying the company of others, eating and watching a movie together. If we want our lives and the message of the Gospel to be relevant to people, we need to engage with their culture - movies, books, music, sports, debate, politics, etc.

Purpose and Play

Some times you need to chat with each other about plans and planning, to evaluate, to challenge etc., but be careful that you aren't getting too serious and only talk 'business' while being together. Make sure you have time for less serious stuff, have time to play and make fun. One golden rule could be: relationships before tasks/activities.

Threats

These are some threats to community life in the western culture. It's important to be aware of:
Consumerism - the church as a kind of shopping mall where you only come to pick up and not to bring, share or reproduce.
Individualism - the trend is that people concentrate more on themselves than on the larger whole of the community they are part of.
(Christian) Dualism - the world is divided into spiritual and worldly. The risk is that we withdraw from the world in our Christian bubble.
Materialism - attaching too much value to items, so that less attention is paid to immaterial things such as relationships.

PRACTICAL EXAMPLES

Please find below some practical examples how you can
start improving your IN relationships and time together.
Watching TV series together.
Go to the playground.
Camping, weekend away.
Go out for a meal.
Playing or watching sports.
Go shopping together.
Grow a community garden together.
Building shared traditions and celebrating.
Bearing burdens.
Helping, serving each other.

Questions:
*How do you do life together (IN) with the people
who are with you, or your community?
How could you implement or improve predicable
and sustainable patterns?*

CHAPTER 10

OUT

In Chapter 1 we looked at the reason for missional discipleship. We've seen that we are part of God's mission and that we have the privilege to join in because of our new identity. So the bottom line is we can't do any kind of OUT apart from our relationship with the Father. It always start with UP. In this Chapter we look at how we can connect and build relationships with people who are not (yet) following Jesus.

IN COMMUNITY

Jesus always sent out his disciples in teams of at least two people. He sent the 72 two-by-two (Luke 10:1) and He even asked two disciples to pick up a donkey (Luke 19:29-30). We are not called to go out on our own. So after UP comes IN. The inward relationships need to lead to our outward relationships.

In our culture it is also a common process that people first belong before they start to believe.
 To experience an authentic community is something people are longing for and this is often a starting point where people open their lives and can take the first steps to believe in God. Often it is all about building relationships. Building relationships with non (not yet) Christians is similar to inviting people in the IN. Just invite people into your ordinary life together. It can be helpful to know where you invite people into.

Sometimes it's not easy to do OUT together, because we are on our own, like in our job or the sports team we're part of. You can make it a kind of a shared OUT when you start praying with others for people you are in contact with. In that way you can share your OUT connections. And why not find someone to join you? For example, if there is an opening at your workplace ask someone from your community to apply for the job. When you play sports try to find someone to join you.

Personal Example:
We've had the privilege that some of us could do things together, sometimes even in the workplace. E.g. Sharon and Simon at their workplace in the hospice. Jacolien and Courtenay who worked both for the Children's Hospital charity. Also Mark was playing soccer together with Simon and Ming.

STRAIGHT FROM THE START

When starting a community it is important that we do OUT from the start as a rhythm. By that we mean that it is important to connect intentionally with non-Christians from the start of the (missional) community. From the gospels it is clear that Jesus started to reach out to the world around him shortly after He called the disciples (see Luke 6:17-19). He didn't wait until the disciples were all convinced He was the son of God but took them immediately with him on mission. How the disciples are involved in the OUT is a gradually growing process until they are send out to make disciples in the world. Then they've become missionaries.

If you start only with UP and IN, e.g. praying together and having a community meal, and not being intentional about going to connect with non-Christians then it will be hard to start with this later on the journey and probably you end up as a small group. We gather together to join in with the mission God has in this world. When it is not clear what our missional focus will be then we could start with a regular activity (rhythm) to start with, for example, serving another group, picking up litter, and getting to know the neighbors. Other examples are: serve at the local food bank or to serve another missional community which already a clear missional goal. Be aware that you are doing this all together. That it is not an option, but part of who you are and what you do as a community.

MISSIONAL VISION AND NATURAL CONNECTION POINT

You need to focus to develop a missional vision. Which means that you know who you're trying to reach. This will help you to be intentional. Often it's one of the following three:
Neighborhood: the area where you live
Network: e.g. sports you are involved in, groups you are a part of, or people you come in contact with
Need: e.g. Food bank, Christians against poverty.

It helps you when you have a natural connection point. With a natural connection point we mean the place where we meet people in a natural way. This could be anywhere. At the office, the gym, college campus, the bar or restaurant, grocery store, or the park.

Lifestyle Versus Activity

OUT is not just doing projects, missional activities or evangelism programs. It is important that we learn to live a missional lifestyle, where mission, evangelism and service are integrated in our daily life. It's not only about making converts, but about making disciples (Matthew 28:19). It isn't a quick fix. We need to make sure that people are being discipled and in turn that they can reproduce themselves.

PEOPLE OF PEACE

For us a very helpful principle is the Person of Peace strategy, where we are looking for the people who are open to us and listen to us. "A person of peace is one who is prepared to hear the message of the Kingdom and the King. He is ready to receive what God will give you to say at that moment."
 It is based on what Jesus says in Luke 10:5-6:
"When you enter a home, greet the family, 'Peace.' If your greeting is received, then it's a good place to stay. But if it's not received, take it back and get out. Don't impose yourself." (MSG).

It can be a relief to know that we don't need to force people to listen. Our job is to look where God is already at work in people's life. It is the job of the Holy Spirit to prepare and convince people. This means we need to pray for 'spiritual eyes' to see where God is at work and how we can join in. Don't impose yourself, or try to force open doors that God has not opened, you may miss the doors God   has opened.

Personal Example:

Our experience is that God often directs us to people we would never have expected. Our first focus was our neighborhood and building relationships there. After doing that for about a year we got to know people in our street by organizing 'parties' (housewarming, holidays, a bonfire, etc.) and inviting people into our home. We didn't do any explicitly Christian events or invite people to church or Bible study. But from the start it was clear to them that we were Christians.

When people started to get to know us and there was an opportunity, we told them we are part of a Christian community and that we wanted to get to know our neighbors and to bless the neighborhood. Having people living with us also made people curious. Simon, who lived with us for two years, was always really open and telling people that he was learning about church without going to the building! We kept on praying about people of peace and started to increase the spiritual atmosphere during our parties, but still we couldn't find someone who wanted to know more about Jesus.

Then Mark and Simon met a student from South Korea on the train. It was his first time in the UK and there was nobody to pick him up from the station, so they offered him a ride. The student had an address, but it was the wrong one. There he stood, late at night, after 15 hours of travelling. and Mark and Simon invited him to come to our house where he could contact his friends. He sorted things out and was able to find the right house that night. As you can imagine he was very grateful he met Mark and Simon. We invited him to come around for dinner the next week and found out he was a Christian. Our first thoughts were 'Great, but we like to meet non-Christians.' But he became part of our small community and connected us with a few other South Korean students who started to come to our 'open meals.' We had a sense that we could invite them to start a Discovery Bible study and they all said yes! In the mean time we met another international student from China who wanted to read the Bible and a colleague of Sharon who is from Iraq also wanted to join. We've started reading the Bible with people we didn't expect!

Bottom line: we were expecting to meet people of peace in our neighborhood, but God brought us internationals. The lesson we've learned is not to be too fixed on a specific group and keep praying for God to lead us to the people of peace. We need to be present in the place where we are and be aware of God's promptings. We need to be bold enough to respond to what God is saying.

Of course this still means we need to find out where people are. Luke 10:5 says "When you enter a home" that means that we get out and meet people! That could mean literally knocking on your neighbors' doors, but it is also about trying to find out if people you meet along the way are open to talking about God.

PASSING AND PERMANENT RELATIONSHIPS

We have learned to make[3] a distinction between two different kind of relationships when we meet people of peace, passing and permanent relationships.

Passing relationships are the people we meet once or twice, e.g. someone we bump into at a store or in the park. We probably won't lead them immediately to Jesus but we can bring them closer. Don't be disappointed when you don't see the result of your short encounter!
I love this Bible verse where the apostle Paul is saying: "I planted the seed, Apollos watered it, but God has been making it grow." (1 Corinthians 3:6). What a relief!

Permanent relationships are family and close friends. It can be people you often spend time with or people you regularly cross paths with at the coffeshop or gym. We may need to wait for a long time before this person becomes a person of peace. It is hard when you want them to get to know Jesus and live in His Kingdom! We need to pray and wait and watch what God is doing. He has the perfect timing. "Be still, and know that I am God" (Psalm 46:10).

PART OF A PROCESS AND NOT AN EVENT

We often want evangelism reduced to a formula we can put into a book and follow it like a recipe, but evangelism is a relational process. It's a process that each one of us worked through ourselves in coming to faith. This helps us to realize when we meet people we need to be patient with those who are not yet ready to receive, and be receptive to noticing those who are. So the OUT is intentionally looking for people who are open and ready to hear about Jesus and to help them in this journey, by inviting them into community life. In Chapter 22 we'll talk more about how we can sow seeds and bring people further in this process.

Questions:
What is God saying/has said about the people (group) you need to reach out to?
What is God (already) doing?
Natural Connection Point - where do you meet them naturally?
Who are your People of Peace? (they like you, listen to you, and serve you)

Our 'Inside Out' Community
We found people of peace in our Hillsborough neighborhood and among Sharon's colleagues at the hospice in the following ways:
We got to know, a South Korean student on the train. He brought a friend, who also brought a friend, who brought two friends. Through another friend we met a Chinese student. Sharon's colleague brought her sister and housemate. They all came first to our community evening on Thursdays and later to Discovery Bible study on Sunday evening. We met people on the street through random encounters and door knocking. We met them at social events and in ourworkplaces. We invited people for pizza nights, drinks and appetizers, bonfire night, a halloween party, to a football watch party, a

pancake breakfast, Christmas caroling, an Easter brunch, watching movies on an outdoor screen, at BBQ's, and through the Korean and Chinese students we met.

STEPPING STONE THREE

CULTURE BEFORE STRUCTURE

70

CHAPTER 11

CHANGING THE CULTURE

As we said in Chapter One, we believe that missional discipleship is a lifestyle. Missional discipleship isn't just doing an activity. It needs to be integrated in our lives so it becomes a natural way of living. When we start thinking how we can create a setting where we can learn this, it's obvious that a new structure alone won't be sufficient, the culture needs to be changed as well. But changing a culture is much harder.

An example in the Old Testament: once Pharaoh allowed the Israelites to leave, it was easy for Moses to get them out of Egypt, but it was much harder to get Egypt out of the Israelites. Out of Egypt they were physically free, but in their minds they were still in Egypt. They needed not only a change of environment but also a shift in their thinking and ideas. It's often similar with discipleship. We could agree that we need to prioritize discipleship, but it's hard to let go of our ideas about how to do church. We need a culture shift. If we don't change our culture, then discipleship probably won't be our number one priority.

Culture is one of the biggest barriers for change. When we would like to have a culture of discipleship and mission we probably need to change the existing culture. The question is: how are we going to do that? But before we dive into changing the culture we need to know what a culture is?

Questions:
Do you have any experience with change? If yes, what is your experience?
Do you tend to focus on structure or culture when you want to change?

WHAT MAKES A CULTURE?

According to the Oxford Dictionary culture is: "the ideas, customs, and social behavior of a particular people." A culture is made up of diverse elements. These can be visible things like behavior and symbols, but also things you don't see immediately, like values and ideas.

When we look at the culture of organizations then we find the so-called 'Onion Model' of Sanders and Neuijen. They say that the culture of an organization consists of the following layers: at the core there are Values and then from the center outwards there are Rituals, Heroes and Symbols.

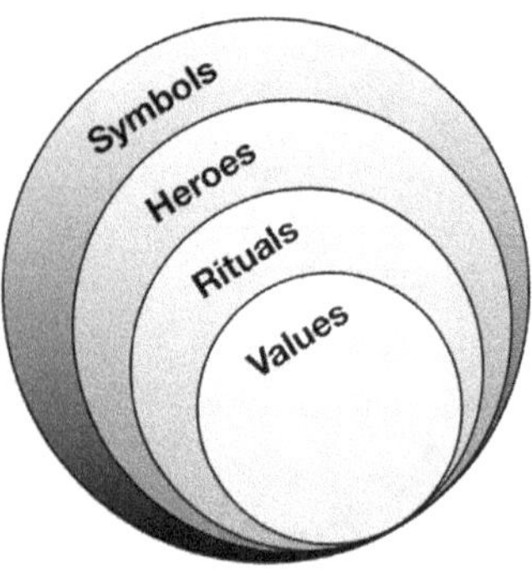

According to Sanders & Neuijen, values are the core of the culture and the most difficult layer to change.

Geert Hofstede says: "During attempts to change cultures new symbols often get a lot of attention; for instance a new name, a new logo, uniforms or advertising slogans and one-liners. All this belongs to the fashionable area of corporate identity. But symbols are no more than the most superficial level of a culture. Without support from more fundamental changes to the heroes, rituals and values of key leaders, new symbols are just a lot of noise which will be silenced quickly". I believe we can learn from this when we want to change the culture in our churches or communities. We won't be successful if we only talk about discipleship, missional lifestyle, new concepts and we come up with a new name for the church/community with promotional materials. Without changes in the shared practices and values of the key leaders we will fail to make a real change.

UNDERLYING BELIEF SYSTEMS

In his book, *On the Verge*, Alan Hirsch writes about underlying belief systems (also called myths or codes) that are deeply rooted and resistant to change. Here are three of the five examples he gives:

- Build it and they will come - This has been a predominant myth over the last fifty years but has deep roots in Christendom thinking. This is one of the lies at the root of what I (Alan Hirsch) have called attractional-extractional church. It has worked for many years, but changing conditions in our context are seriously challenging its viability.
- We need clergy, buildings, and Sunday services in order to be a real church - Again we can see the predominantly institutional paradigm impressing itself on our imaginations here. But this myth cannot explain the very best, and most impactful, Christian movements in history - which are often persecuted (therefore underground and without buildings) and are patently not run by seminary-trained professionals. Yet the myth persists even in contemporary churches; for example, we say it's "pastor so-and-so's church" and we "go to church" (meaning the building). Ask most people what ministry is and they will say it's something the clergy do. If the people have anything at all to do with it, it's seen as volunteering for something and it's temporary. This myth is very deeply embedded into our codes, and we have to deliberately recode it before we can advance to becoming an apostolic movement.
- We are a Bible-teaching church - The subtext here is that if we simply teach more Bible (and teach it better), things will automatically change. The reality is that this is far from the truth. The Western church has more theology, commentaries, training, and intellectual tradition than any other time in history, and it certainly hasn't produced the desired revival - perhaps it has even influenced the opposite! This is not to say we ought to be biblically illiterate, but we must remember we are perfectly designed to produce what we are currently producing. I (Alan Hirsch) am sorry to say this, but more beautifully delivered three-point sermons are not going to solve your missional problems - or any serious strategic problems, for that matter! If they could do that, we would be there now. Remember, the Pharisees knew their Scriptures better than anyone and missed the whole point of God in Jesus (Matt 23:24; John 5:39-40).

If we only change the things we can see and do what we can achieve quickly then we probably won't change the culture.

E.g. if you merge two small groups and call them a missional community, but you don't change their values and rituals, then the former small groups will hardly operate as a missional community.

When we only change the structure, people will go back to what they once knew when they experience challenge and or hard times (the law of institutional/religious gravity). We are looking for a cultural change which goes deeper. What makes this approach hard is that it isn't a quick fix, nor is it always visible.
It is like an iceberg where about 80% is under the surface.

Organized / Structured
(small group,
missional community)

Organic / Spontaneous
Access to Leader's life

It's interesting what Jesus said about the Kingdom: "The kingdom of God is not coming with things that can be observed; nor will they say, 'Look, here it is!' or 'There it is!' For, in fact, the kingdom of God is among you." Luke 17:20-21

Questions:
What is your Kairos?

Which of these myths do you recognize?

Are these myths holding you back in changing the culture? If yes, which one, how and why?

Is there a value you may need to let go of?

What are values you value? What do you celebrate? E.g. conversions, baptisms, 3rd generation dsciples?

Where is the structure not supporting the culture?

What is the culture you would like to see? And which core beliefs you think are important?

AN EXAMPLE OF A DISCIPLESHIP CULTURE ONION

When we use the Onion model for a discipleship culture it could look like this:

Values:
- We are all disciples and learners.
- Failing is part of the discipling process and it's ok as long as we learn from it.
- We regularly encourage each other.
- Process rather than a structured program.
- Quality before quantity - you can only disciple a few.
- Walk your talk - practice what you preach - integrity.
- High on accountability and low on control.
- We always look for how we can do multiplication.
- The Sunday gathering is not enough for a discipleship process.
- Leaders go first.

Rituals:
- Rhythms in terms of UP (relationship with God) IN (relationships with fellow Christians) and OUT (relationships with non-Christians).
- A practice of apprenticeship or immersion which is key for a good discipleship process.

Heroes:
- Jesus.
- Biblical characters, like the disciples and Paul.
- Good role models or spiritual parents.
- Think also of 'missional models' who are not Christian.

Symbols:
- Name of a church or community
- Using specific language and words (e.g. Triangle, Circle, Person of Peace, Family on Mission, etc.).

Patience and Practice

In this proces of changing the culture we need patience and practice. We need to lay down our own expectations about how quick change can happen. You don't change a culture overnight. What can help the process is that the new culture becomes visible, it needs to be practised. The best way to do that is the visionary/apostle/pioneer/leader goes first. He/she needs to give an example which people can imitate.

In many cases we will challenge existing practices and/or values. For a leader this could mean that some people don't want to follow and will leave. This is disappointing, but is part of the cost. Therefore it's wise to think carefully about your pace, how fast you want to go and how radical you want to be.

Question:
Where do you need to go first?

THE BELL CURVE OF WILLINGNESS TO CHANGE

If you want to change the culture of an existing group you need to be wise. Two of my (Mark) biggest mistakes was that I believed everybody would agree change was necessary and be willing to change. I assumed the whole group was homogeneous and treated them as such. The reality was the majority didn't feel the need to change and the group wasn't homogeneous. Later I discovered about The Bell Curve of Willingness to Change[1] which I found very helpful. The main idea is to distinguish the following 5 groups of people:

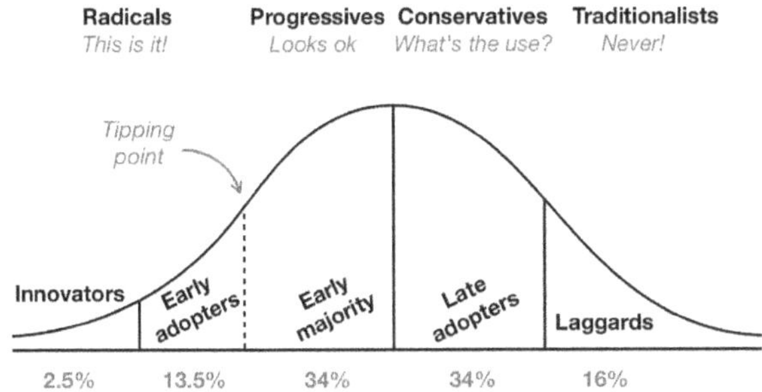

1. Innovators

- Have a great interest in new ideas and a desire to be daring and risky
- Can cope with uncertainty regarding change
- May not be respected by other members of the organization

2. Early Adopters

- Are the critical group for change/opinion leaders
- Contain role models for others that respect them for judicious 'innovation decisions'
- Are not too far ahead of the organization as compared to innovators
- Decrease uncertainty when they adopt new ideas

3. Early Majority

- Adopt new ideas before the average members of the organization
- Not opinion leaders, they make decisions slowly and carefully
- Follow with deliberate willingness in adopting change but rarely lead

4. Late Majority

- Adopt innovations after the majority of the organization
- Generally are skeptical and cautious
- Respond to pressure from their peers and new organizational norms

5. Laggards

- Are isolated and interact with others with traditional values
- Usually make decisions on what has been done in the past
- Possess almost no opinion leaders
- Often are suspicious of change and change agents

---

1   Rogers, E. M. & Shoemaker, F. F., *Communication of Innovation.* New York: The Free Press, (1971).

A STRATEGY FOR CHANGE

- Start to find out where people are in this bell curve (this is not about making a distinction between good and bad).
- Start with the early adopters or people of peace (who are open to you and your ideas).
- They will connect with the early majority and the early majority will connect with the late majority.
- The tipping point is around 15%, after this it will go naturally.
- Make sure people will have the opportunity to experience it, so you need to start modelling it.
- Don't spend too much time on laggards, it sounds harsh but they won't listen to Innovators.

Questions:
What is God saying to you?
What is your response?

CHAPTER 12

A LEARNING CULTURE

A disciple is a learner. A discipleship culture is a culture of learning where we grow in following Jesus. One of the challenges we face is the way we learn to follow Jesus. In our churches often there is an emphasis on giving people the 'right' information. Mostly done via the method of lecture (oral presentation). But when we look at how Jesus discipled his students we see a different approach. Although He teaches his disciples, He also gave them the opportunity to observe, ask questions, discuss, apply to their lives, and receive feedback. This is an ongoing growth process. As disciples we need to keep on learning and growing. It isn't a program with an instant solution. It is a lifestyle and it will take time.

So when we look at discipleship, learning to become more like Jesus, we need to ask ourselves: "What is it what we need to learn?" Is it only a set of beliefs or knowledge that makes us a follower of Jesus or do we need to learn some practical skills (behavior) as well? If so, how can we gain those practical skills? Probably it is both!

We need to practice if we want to learn to pray, pray for others, heal and deliver people. Similarly, we need concrete examples of reaching out to people, telling our story, explaining the Gospel, hearing God, learning to trust God etc. Wouldn't it be great if we could have practical learning opportunities for all people in our churches and communities?

INFORMATION-IMITATION-INNOVATION

For too long we have discipled people in only one way: by giving information. The assumption was (and often still is) if we teach the Bible or when we give a course about ... (you name it) then people will change (innovation application) and become more like Jesus. We have found that only teaching and offering discipleship courses doesn't produce ongoing transformation in people's life (application). Why not? We learn by doing. Most people don't learn via reading a book and then doing. Would you like to be operated on by a doctor who has only learned by reading books? We need a process, relationships with people we can follow and learn from, and opportunities to step out and try things.

Learning also means we make mistakes. We learn the most from our errors! We live in a culture of instant solutions and perfectionism. Perseverance and being vulnerable about our mistakes is difficult, but we need this if we want to learn and grow as disciples. In the business world this is a well-known principle. Bill Gates says the following about failures: "It is fine to celebrate success, but it is more important to heed the lessons of failure"[2] and "Success is a lousy teacher. It seduces smart people into thinking they can't lose."[3]

We need churches and communities who embody this learning environment. We need a learning environment which is connected with and integrated in our daily lives. We have found this tool to be so helpful in clarifying the relationship between information, imitation, and innovation:

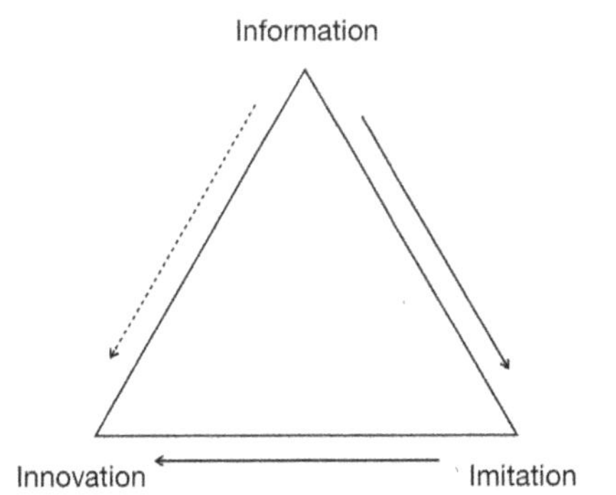

---

2 https://www.brainyquote.com/quotes/quotes/b/billgates385735.html

3 https://www.brainyquote.com/quotes/quotes/b/billgates122131.html

Giving information is not bad and is part of the process, but it isn't the whole picture. In 1 Corinthians 4:16-17 Paul says: "I urge you to imitate me. That is why I have sent you Timothy, my beloved and faithful child in the Lord. He will remind you of my way of life in Christ Jesus, ..." and in 1 Corinthians 11:1 "Follow my example, as I follow the example of Christ."
Paul is saying is that, despite his imperfections, he is a role model for people to learn how to follow Jesus.

IMITATION

Two ways we can use the principle of a role model is apprenticeship and immersion. Both give an opportunity to learn from people who are experienced in areas the disciples want to grow by simply imitating them.

- Apprenticeship gives you the opportunity to imitate someone and learn the skills you want to learn by practical hands-on experience, often offered in a structured way.
- Immersion happens when you have the opportunity to absorb yourself in a culture where the things you want to learn are part of everyday life. It is less structured and often more spontaneous.

Key in both of these is access to the discipler/leader's life (both quality and quantity). Jesus did not disciple people for one hour on Tuesday night. It took him 3 years of 24/7 engagement to disciple a bunch of guys.

Similar to changing the culture we can use the metaphor of an iceberg. The tendency is to focus only on the structured part of discipleship, which is above the surface. This can be teaching input, regular meetings with your missional community, structured mentoring, etc. While the bigger part is under the surface, often not seen and organic instead of structured.

LEARNER BEFORE LEADER

The first important step in creating a culture of learning is being part of a discipleship process yourself. You can't lead people where you've never been yourself. Many people aren't discipled and don't have an example of being discipled intentionally. If we want to make disciples who make disciples we need to be a disciples first. A phrase we've heard a lot during our time in Sheffield is this: "A disciple is meant to look like a shepherd from the back and a sheep from the front."

Each disciple is in a learning process. This starts with listening to the words of Jesus and obeying the things He says. A disciple is someone who follows Jesus in words and deeds. By responding to what God says, we get closer to Christ and grow in our understanding of His love for us. From this place of love we learn to love one another and the world around us. This process of listening and responding is about becoming more and more like Jesus in our character and competencies. It is a process, not a program. It is a process of transformation!

In John 5:19 Jesus says: "the Son can do nothing by himself; he can do only what he sees his Father doing, because whatever the Father does the Son also does." So for us it also starts by going to God and listening for what He is saying and doing.

- Jesus promises by his Holy Spirit to be with us. "I am with you always, to the very end of the age." (Matthew 28:20)
- The Holy Spirit strengthens us. "I pray that out of his glorious riches he may strengthen you with power through his Spirit in your inner being, so that Christ may dwell in your hearts through faith." (Ephesians 3:16-17)

Being a disciple is not just knowing the words of Jesus, but living by these words, following these words, following the Master in what He says and does. A disciple does not learn theory without obligation, but surrenders himself to be shaped by Jesus. A disciple is not just a student who agrees with the Master's teachings, but follows the Master's practice of life. Dietrich Bonhoeffer, a well-known German pastor, also says that the Christian faith is not only the adoption of a concept or idea about Christ. He calls this cheap grace. That's grace without imitation, grace without the cross, grace without the living, incarnate Jesus Christ. It is all about costly grace when we listen to the call of Jesus and follow him. Following is also obeying, taking decisive steps. Belief and obedience have everything to do with each other. Bonhoeffer concludes that both statements are true "Only he who believes is obedient, and only he who is obedient believes." [4]

---

4 D. Bonhoeffer, *The Cost of Discipleship.* p.69

CHAPTER 13

A NEW STRUCTURE

We want to see disciples who make disciples who make disciples, right? To create an environment where that can take place we need to not only change the culture (see Chapter 11), but also change the structure. A Sunday gathering is great for corporate worship and teaching, but it isn't efficient for all discipleship. We don't say that Sunday gatherings are a bad thing to do, but if we think discipleship is the key, we need to start prioritizing it and create a setting where discipleship can thrive.

KNOWN VERSUS NEW

If we look at church as we know it then we will probably recognize some of the following activities:
Weekly or bi-weekly: Sunday services, midweek gatherings for the core group, small groups, Bible studies, children's ministry, meetings for teenagers, students, young adults, and an occassional training course. To keep this going we need resources: people, time and money.

When discipleship is the main thing then we need to organize things differently. We need imitation and immersion to disciple people well. This will affect how we organize church and how our resources will be spent.

We need to create a setting where we have time to invest in disciples, where the number of disciples are limited, and where there is a safe place to practice what people have learned. To do this we need smaller settings like extended families. The main goal of a family is to raise children, who then become mature adults who can create a family who raise children, who then become mature adults.

You can call these smaller settings extended families, oikos, missional community, faith communities etc., but the principles are the same. Such a community needs to be:
- Missional - Part of God's mission to restore relationships between God and people.
- Formational - Making disciples; creating a place where people can learn and be immersed in the culture.
- Ecclesial - Part of a local expression of church - UP-IN-OUT.
- Contextual - Connecting with the target group they feel called to reach.

Temple and Homes

When we look at Acts 2, we see people coming together in their houses as well as in the Temple - there is a place for both. "Every day they continued to meet together in the temple courts. They broke bread in their homes and ate together with glad and sincere hearts." (Acts 2:46)

We need a balance between community gatherings and corporate celebrations (Although you can only organize a big gathering when you have a certain number of people).

Sustainable Rhythms

It's important to make the rhythms sustainable, so that you can build and maintain momentum. You need to make sure there is enough space and energy for people to connect with people outside the church, to do OUT.

HOW TO START A NEW STRUCTURE

Although every situation is different, in general we distinguish a few phases which people go through when starting to live missionally with others.

Phase 1, Missional Disciple: It starts with someone who has a vision or a calling. This vision must be part of the Great Commission of making disciples. That person realizes they need others to help them to make that vision real, so they gather others to join him/her (number of people: 1 - 2).

Phase 2, Extended Family/Missional House: one way to start is to invite family members to join, or to invite others to come to live in the same area or house. If you are intentional about living missionally with a few people in the same house, we call it a missional house. If not, you can call it an extended family (number of people: 3 - 15, singles, couples, kids/no kids).

Phase 3, Missional Community: When you invite more people to join you in mission and they don't live in the same house we call it a missional community (number of people: 15 - 30).

Phase 4, Community of Communities or Church Plant: The final phase is when there are several missional communities that have grown from each other. Together you form a big community or church plant (number of people: 60 - 120).

Question:
Are you more comfortable with gatherings in the Temple setting or the Home setting?

What setting will allow for more immersion and imitation?

Do you feel you are at Phase 1, Phase 2, Phase 3, or Phase 4?

CHAPTER 14

RHYTHMS OF LIFE

There are two principles in the Bible which help us to set fruitful rhythms and embrace the seasons of life. They both are illustrated in the Semi-Circle.

- Rest and Work
- Pruning and Fruitfulness

The first one we will consider is the Semi-Circle of rest and work. We need to have a healthy rhythm of rest and work if we want to be healthy. This rhythm is something we can choose to plan into our lives in response to the Word. Probably everybody would agree on that, but for lots of people it can be hard to rest well.

The second one is the Semi-Circle of pruning and fruitfulness. This rhythm is not a rhythm that we can choose and plan intentionally. Often pruning happens to us and can be painful as well, but we'll see that it is a natural rhythm. Before we take a look at the Semi-Circle of pruning and fruitfulness, we'll start with rest and work.

REST AND WORK

Why do we need rest? Rest is important. God himself rested from His work. "By the seventh day God had finished the work he had been doing; so on the seventh day he rested from all his work". (Genesis 2:2) It's so important that rest is a commandment (4th) given by God to his people: "Remember the Sabbath day by keeping it holy. Six days you shall labor and do all your work, but the seventh day is a sabbath to the Lord your God." (Exodus 20:8).

Sabbath means rest. Having this day of rest was a gift to the people of Israel, no other nation had the privilege of a day of rest, but they needed to trust God that He provides enough for seven days. Rest was also important for Jesus as He took time out to rest alone or

with his disciples.

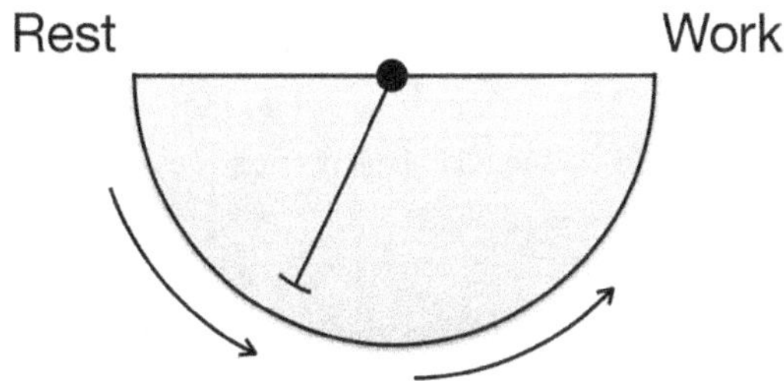

Healthy rhythms starts with rest. It is a reminder of the principle of the flow of grace: grace flows from our relationship with God (UP) to our relationships to each other (IN) and from there (OUT) to people who don't know him.

In the garden of Eden, God walked in the cool of the day with Adam and Eve. Their relationship flowed out of their relationship with him and it was from this place of rest that they were called to rule over the earth. If grace is to flow into the work we are called to, it needs to start in a place of rest with the Father and enjoyment of the family (in the wider sense) that He has given us. So we see that creating a healthy rhythm of rest and work is very much related to the UP-IN-OUT Triangle.

To achieve balance in our rhythm of rest and work we will have to be intentional because:

- God has left it to us to choose to rest
- We live in a society which values productivity above leisure
- We will all have internal barriers that often create a resistance to the order of rest and work God has given us

If we need to be intentional about rest, we need to know what rest is for us and for the people in our families and communities.

Identify What Is Rest and What Is Work

Rest doesn't mean doing nothing. Rest or recreation has

two facets:
- Activities that require no effort (reduced energy levels) - like reading, listening to music, meal out with spouse, sleeping on on a Saturday morning, watching a TV series
- Activities that recreate us but do require effort, a cycle ride, a long hike, having friends over for a barbecue, going to a party

What gives us rest and recreates us will be different depending on our personality type and calling. E.g. an extravert is unlikely to feel as reenergized by two days alone reading and listening to music as an introvert might. And your Fivefold gifting may affect what is rest for you as well (see Sharon's personal example).

Personal Examples:

Mark: I am an introverted thinker and I need regular time on my own. I love to hang out with people, both Christians and non-Christians, but to be present I need to charge my batteries beforehand. My ideal Saturday is to have a chunk of time with nothing planned and time on my own.

Sharon: I am an evangelist/teacher in the fivefold. Even though I am an extrovert and often reenergized around people I can find it draining to be in social situations with people who don't know Jesus. Especially if they are not people of peace because my heart is constantly looking for the opportunity to share with them and I am holding back and monitoring my communication. This is actually work nor rest although to other extroverts it could be recreation. So typically rest may be reading, listening to music, going out for a meal, hanging out with friends.

Exercise

Make lists of what is actually rest for you. Alone, with a member of your family, with your nuclear family or household, with your closest disciples, with your community. This will help you build your rhythms of rest and work in the context of leading others in this.

INTERNAL RESISTANCE

Knowing what rest is, is not enough. We need to make sure we actually have rest. We need to put it into practice, which can be hard sometimes. Therefore we need to address any internal resistance we have, so that we can embrace a lifestyle of rest and work. As we have seen before (in Chapter 3) we tend to fall into three main internal traps which affect our thinking and actions. These are Approval, Appetite and Ambition. Each of these can set us up to an internal struggle that will undermine any plans to really follow Jesus' example in this area. We use again the temptations triangle which we used in Chapter 3.

Approval

We struggle with the lies that 'we are only ok if we are sure people see us as: lovable, successful or unique'. This sets us up to embrace a life where we can't say no and need to be busy helping people, or (striving) to be successful. We may also fall into the trap of pulling away from others, and trying to prove that we are different by going deeper and deeper into the work that is unique to us. Alternatively we may find it hard to start projects for fear we will upset others or that they will fail or just because we don't want to do what others are doing.

All these issues are related to not trusting that our Father really loves us and approves of us unconditionally.

Truth: I'm ok because the Father loves me in just the same way He loves Jesus.

Appetite

We struggle with the lie that we are only ok if we can provide for ourselves and if we do not, we will be depleted and lacking, insecure and bereft of joy. This sets us up for a life where we can be afraid of work depleting our resources. We can regard work as a burden and a threat to our freedom.

So there can be barriers to work but more commonly we struggle with the barriers to rest. At times we will use work as a way to retreat from the unpredictable demands of everyday life and relationships. We can be afraid to stop because we think we need to have every issue covered to be secure and to be financially secure, or we may have such a buzz from the ideas and opportunities that our work affords that we neglect to rest.

All these issues are rooted in a lack of trust that God will provide and a failure to ask the Holy Spirit to fill us providing all that we need.
Truth: I'm ok because the Spirit fills me to overflowing and provides all that my heart needs.

Ambition

We struggle with the lie that we are masters of our own destiny and that of others. We think that if we do not take control and maintain it we will be powerless, unheard and dominated or have failed and deserve punishment. We try to take control over ourselves rather than submitting to the one who is sovereign. This sets us up for struggles with rest and work. We may resist work that is delegated by others, that requires us to step out of our comfort zone or that we may fail at. That being said, our greater challenge is often to let go of control for a time and rest. We think that if we are not working others will take over what is our domain, we will not be able to regain the motivation or energy to start again or that if we let go of control others will not achieve our standards and the work will fail. And then we will have failed.

All these issues are rooted in our desire to take control and are only dealt with as we submit control to the the King who gave up his control to give us His life, peace and righteousness. It is His Kingdom not ours that we are investing in.
Truth: I am ok because I'm following the King of life, peace and righteousness.

The rest & work Semi-Circle requires that we choose to trust and plan rest and work intentionally. And It's important that we see rest not only as a spiritual thing. It starts with physical rest. Without the physical rest it's hard to rest spiritually.

Questions:

How easy or hard is it for you to rest?

Which of these barriers (approval, appetite and ambition) resonates with you?

What are the ungodly beliefs?

What is a truth which you can use to replace the lie?

Assignment

Take a one-week period and track how every hour is spent.

How are you investing time, energy and resources?

How intentional are you?

Are you aware of the return you are looking for?

What's the connection between the first two questions?

Make an inventory of what is rest and work for you remembering that for you a party may be work and designing a front cover for a flyer may actually be recreational.

Make a plan for rest and work for the next month.

PRUNING AND FRUITFULNESS

The second Semi-Circle is the rhythm of abiding, growing, fruitfulness and pruning. It's based on: John 15:1-2, The Vine and the Branches: "I am the true vine, and my Father is the gardener. He cuts off every branch in me that bears no fruit, while every branch that does bear fruit He prunes so that it will be even more fruitful."

This is not a rhythm that we can choose and plan intentionally. Although we need to choose to abide, often pruning happens to us. When we find that what we do no longer flourishes, that things we value are taken from us, or that we feel like we are dry and our spiritual life feels dead, we can look to this principle and ask, "Am I being pruned?"

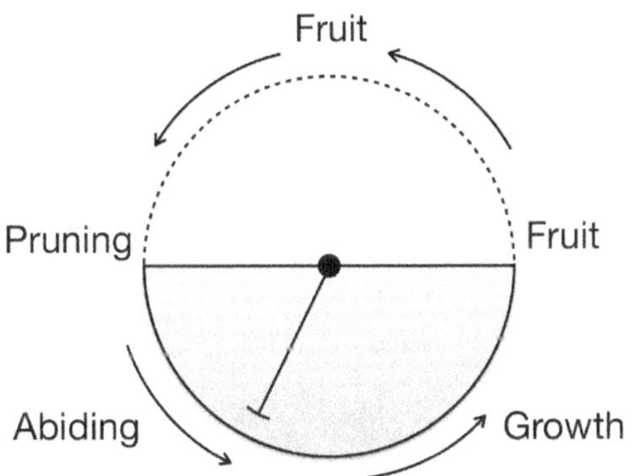

The key words of this rhythm are Trust, Surrender and Embrace.
Pruning is part of our (spiritual) lives. For me (Mark) it helps to know that there's a reason for pruning, which is to be even more fruitful. Note: God prunes the fruitful branches.

Biblical Examples:

Joseph - Potiphar's house, in prison then ruling the whole kingdom.
Moses - prince of Egypt, exile, leader of a nation.
Jesus - heaven, pruning in a manger, adulthood,

temptations, fruitful, cross, resurrection, the church is born.

Signs of Pruning

There are some signs which can be recognised as pruning:

- More effort produces less fruit.
- A feeling of dryness and distance from God.
- Things we value are taken from us.
- Opportunities dry up.
- Areas of personal struggle that we have previously experienced victory in once more become a struggle.
- Gifts we have taken for granted seem to disappear.
- Areas of fruitfulness taken away.

Note: Cutting dead or unfruitful branches is not pruning.

Dying to Self, Ready for Resurrection

When we find ourselves in seasons of disappointment, loss of influence, authority, reputation, freedom, autonomy, finances, relationships we have a choice: do we try to save our lives or do we allow ourselves to die? Do we try to hold on to these things or do we return to our Father and ask him to hide us in Him and leave Him to vindicate us and provide for us? Do we forgive and take the way of the cross trusting Him and leaning on Him?

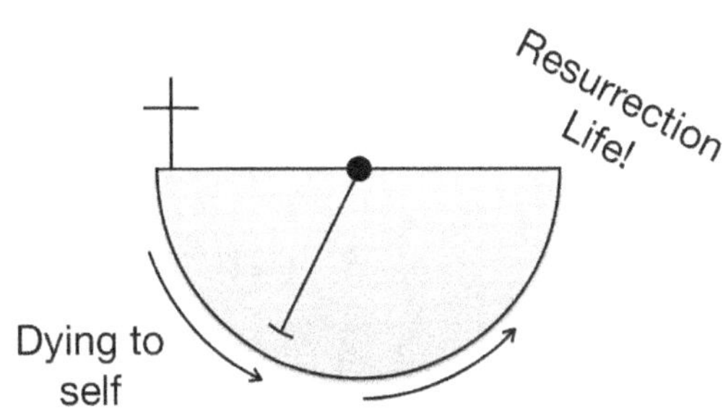

Understanding these rhythms can encourage us that if we embrace pruning and even death to self we will see fruitfulness and resurrection. Paul writes the following about Jesus: "He did not think equality with God was something to cling to, instead he humbled himself in obedience to God and died a criminals death on a cross. Therefore God elevated him to the highest honour and gave him a name above all names." (Philippians 2:5-9) And Luke writes: "If you cling to your life you will lose it, but if you let your life go you will save it." (Luke 17:33) If you are experiencing loss and brokenness, you need to ask if this is a time to allow your own agenda to die. Is this a time to lay down your feelings, will, and demands? Do you need to submit to 'dying' and allow God to bring resurrection in His time? Both pruning and dying require us to draw closer to God.

Questions:
Do you recognize these phases in areas of your life (past or present)?
In what phase do you think you are know?
What is your automatic response when you face pruning?

STEPPING STONE FOUR

VISION & CALLING

90

CHAPTER 15

VISION

Discuss: What do you think vision is?

According to the Oxford Dictionary vision is: "The ability to think about, or plan, the future with imagination or wisdom. The ability to see beyond the present, the physical or experienced."[1]

For some people the word vision can be overwhelming. If so, think about what your passion is and what do you want to see happen?

WHY DO YOU NEED VISION?

Where there is vision there is:
- Shared direction, focus, and unity of choices.
- Energy towards the same goals.
- The continuous involvement of new people.
- Effective sharing of tasks and responsibilities.
- Sacrifice short-term convenience for long term gains.
- Common reference point for resolving conflict.
- A new hope, new life, and a new sense of victory.

On the other hand where there is no vision:
- Ministry is likely to be reactive and short-term.
- There will be conflicts of expectation and direction.
- Cooperative work is difficult.
- Everyone does their own thing.

Biblical Examples of Vision

Here are some biblical examples of vision and the people who are called to make it happen:
- People of Israel physically liberated from slavery, living in freedom: Moses
- Take possession of the promised land: Joshua
- A king who is following God: David
- People living in spiritual freedom, train the first group: Jesus

- Proclamation of the name of God to the Gentiles (Rom 1:5): Saul/Paul
- Multiplying Jesus followers: Disciples

WHO NEEDS VISION?

Question:

Who do you think needs a vision? And why?

Basically everyone needs vision. This is not just for the big and famous leaders. This great mission is for every follower of Jesus: "Therefore, go and make disciples of all the nations, baptizing them in the name of the Father and the Son and the Holy Spirit and teaching them to obey everything I commanded you. And surely I am with you always, to the very end of the age." (Matthew 28:19). This is the great commission and the big vision from God for this world. A true disciple is the one who is hearing this and is listening to God and knows that

---

1 http://www.oxforddictionaries.com/definition/english/vision

their destiny is to make a difference in God's Kingdom and the world. The question is to find out how we can step into this vision and what that looks like in our daily ordinary lives.

Five Important Things

There are five important things we think you need to know:

1. We believe that God is the giver of a vision. And in that case it's never 'my' vision, but God's vision for me, or God's calling for that specific vision. ("For we are God's workmanship, created in Christ Jesus to do good works, which God prepared in advance for us to do." Ephesians 2:10)

2. A vision is never meant for one specific person, He'll always give a shared vision. Think about it: what would it look like if everybody had his or her own vision?

3. Vision is different from calling. David had a vision of a temple, yet he wasn't called by God to build it ("But the Lord said to my father David, 'Because it was in your heart to build a temple for my Name, you did well to have this in your heart. Nevertheless, you are not the one to build the temple, but your son, who is your own flesh and blood—he is the one who will build the temple for my Name.'" - 1 Kings 8:18-19). It was his son Solomon who God called to build it. However David did contribute by making all kind of arrangements.

4. A vision doesn't have to be big. You can receive a vision to invest in other people, which could mean invite them into your life to disciple them.

5. When you receive a vision often it's not really clear how to get there. Our experience is that God is showing us only the next step to get there and not the total plan how to accomplish it. We need to pray about that next step and the direction. It could be that the logical next step is flowing out of the things we're already doing.

HOW DO YOU GET VISION?

It starts when you believe that God can and wants to do something great with your life. You must believe what God has for you. The promises of God are for everyone who puts their trust in Him and follows His wisdom. When God created men, he gave them authority to rule. (Gen 1:26-28). Your authority is only going to work if you use your God-given gifts and talents for the sake of this world and other people.

So it is not all about us, but it is about being passionate in what God is passionate, and to love one another.

"Love the Lord your God with all your heart, and with all your soul, and with all your mind. This is the first and greatest commandment. And the second is like it, 'Love your neighbor as yourself'" (Matthew 22:37-40). That means to unselfishly seek the best or higher good for other (AMP).

- willing to listen
- willing to wait - being patience

There are four practical ways of how we receive vision, and it's good to know that it can be a combination of two or more:

- Revelation
- Holy discontent
- Heart's desire
- Following and joining someone else's vision

Revelation

As we've seen in Chapter 8, we can receive a word or picture from God. There are quite a few people in the Bible who heard the audible voice of God speaking them. E.g. Noah, Abraham and Paul. God is still speaking, but hearing the audible voice of God is something that hasn't happened to me yet. The way I typically hear from God is through a sense, a picture, a word from the Bible, etc. We all can receive revelation by listening to God and receiving a sense, a word or a Bible verse. "The sheep that are My own hear My voice and listen to Me; I know them, and they follow Me." - John 10:27 (AMP)

The 'raw' material (words, pictures, dreams etc) we call revelation and this needs weighing and discernment. Especially when this is about a (new) vision for our life and ministry. We need to involve trustworthy people in our lives and community or church to process this with. This discerning process is something we talk about later in this session.

It is quite common for God to reveal a 'big' vision, but we don't see how to get there. Our experience is that God likes us to be dependent on him and other people to figure out how to get there. We need faith to trust Him in every step we take. With every step we take, He is leading us closer and closer to the vision He has for our lives. It is important to have other Christians in our lives who are helping us to discern what God is saying to us and it can be a challenge to find these people and to open up our lives to them. But we believe and have seen God's provision to give wise people and connections who are willing to journey with us and who hold us accountable.

Personal Example:

Years ago Mark and I (Jacolien) both had a sense that the church needs a reformation and that discipleship and mission would be the key to that reformation. We also received a prophetic word from someone who didn't know us, which was about being involved in a world-wide movement. At the time we really didn't know what to do with that, but we wrote it down and prayed about it. Looking back we can see that God has led us to be connected with the right people who helped us to work out what this could look like. By his grace He guided every step to the place where we are now. Starting to live a missional lifestyle in community and to train other young people fits the vision God gave us years ago. We don't think we're done yet, rather it is something that started ten years ago and is still a work in progress!

Question:

Have you received any words or pictures about vision? If so, how do/did you process these?

Holy Discontent

What do we see that creates so much angst, and anxiety, and frustration in us? What is it that creates an internal firestorm, and pushes an activism button in us that makes us say, "That's all I can stand. God you can use me, but I can't stand this any more." This is holy discontent; something you have a difficult time seeing, hearing, or feeling without doing something about it.

Two biblical examples of people with a holy discontent are Moses and Nehemiah.

- One day, after Moses had grown up, he went out to where his own people were and watched them at their hard labor. He saw an Egyptian beating a Hebrew, one of his own people. Looking this way and that and seeing no one, he killed the Egyptian and hid him in the sand. (Exodus 2:11-12)

- "They said to me, "Those who survived the exile and are back in the province are in great trouble and disgrace. The wall of Jerusalem is broken down, and its gates have been burned with fire." When I heard these things, I sat down and wept. For some days I mourned and fasted and prayed before the God of heaven." (Nehemiah 1: 3-4)

We need to ask God and others if our holy discontent is in line with what God wants to change in this world. It is about bringing God's justice and righteousness, not about our own frustration or longing to have things right (see Chapter 17).

Heart's Desire

Where a holy discontent can be a negative motivation, God can stir something positive as well. This is what He says in His word:
"May He grant you according to your heart's desire, and make all your plans succeed." (Psalm 20:4 NLT)
"Trust in the LORD, and do good. then you will live safely in the land and prosper. Take delight in the Lord and He will give you your heart's desires." (Psalm 37:3-5 NLT)

This can be a dream and desire we have and not primarily based on a revelation or word we've received from God. This doesn't mean that this is wrong, but again it is important to bring our desires and dreams to God to ask him to sanctify them. We need to be willing to be clay in the hand of our Master. He is the who can form our desires into desires of his heart!

An example of a heart's desire is King David, "But the Lord said to my father David 'Because it was in your heart to build a temple for my Name, you did well to have it in your heart to build me a temple for my Name." (1 Kings 8:18)

Following and Joining Someone Else's Vision

Not everyone needs to come up with their own vision. Vision can also be joining in with an existing vision. This can easily be overlooked. We live in an individualistic world where everyone needs to be self-sufficient, but stepping into what God has for us always involves other people. The key is that we don't have a vision and calling on our own. Not everyone can have a vision on their own. This means most of the time people with a vision need to cast their vision and invite others to join them. In reality we've seen that quite a few people like to follow someone else's vision and help him or her make that vision a reality. This means some people need to accept that they don't have to come with vision and may even feel relieved about that. There is tendency, also in today's church culture, that it is all about the visionairies and explorers. We all need to learn to serve one another and this could mean that joining and following someone's else vision is what God is calling us to do.

Personal Example:

Mark - I've worked quite a few years as an associate pastor under the leadership of a board of elders and was following the vision of the church. There was space to develop my 'personal' vision, but this was always part of the bigger vision. Also when I've worked for 3DM in the UK it meant that I was following and joining someone else's vision although it had a lot of overlap with my vision. It was good to learn how to serve and I'm convinced it will help me to fulfill my God-given vision.

Questions:
Does one of the four ways to receive a vision resonate with you? Which one?
Do you have a holy discontent or heart's desire? How do you process that?
Are you following or joining in someone else's vision? Or do you like someone else's vision?

SHARED VISION AND DIFFERENCES

It is important to have a shared vision, especially as a married couple because you 'are one'. If you have two separate visions the tendency is that you'll start doing your own thing, while you need one another.

Our experiences with couples is that often one of them is a big-picture-vision person while the other is more a here-and-now vision person. Both have a vision and it's not about good and bad, because it's the way we're wired. The challenge however is how can we celebrate our differences and support one another. Big picture people need people who help them practically, otherwise they live in their future vision and nothing happens in the present. People who tend to live in the present sometimes need a bigger picture challenge to become more intentional. We can have a tendency to surround ourselves with people who are the same, but we need both perspectives when we start stepping into our vision.

Personal Example:

Mark's vision has grown from a holy discontent about discipleship and mission in the church. Together with Jacolien he did some research for our theological study and found out that discipleship was not really functioning in the churches in the Netherlands. They both have a heart to help the churches in the Western world. What we'd like to see is that ordinary Christians are equipped to live a missional lifestyle in community, know how to reach out to people, and disciple them so they multiply themselves. This is a vision with communities of practitioners throughout Europe where people are being discipled on the ground (apprenticeship or immersion) and sent out to do the same. Jacolien is joining Mark's vision and basically it's a shared vision.

Another vision that is connected with this is about being spiritual parents. In the last few years when people prayed for us we've received many prophetic words about being spiritual parents. We've processed these by writing them down and talking about it with others. Our circumstance of not having biological children and confirmation of others helped us have faith that this could be a vision for us to step into. When Sharon asked us to form a missional household and to live together with younger people to disciple them, everything fell into place.

PRACTICAL EXERCISES

A. If you don't have vision yet, please answer the following questions:

We talked about four ways that God gives vision (revelation, hearts desire, holy discontent or joining someone else's vision). If you have a sense God has already given you some kind of vision or direction, can you describe it and tell to which one of the four it is related? (It's ok if it isn't clear yet).

Passion - what is your passion? What are you passionate about?

Possessions - what are the resources you have? (time, experiences, knowledge, training etc)

Problems - what are the problems in your neighborhood or network? Or is there a need to fulfill?

Where are the opportunities to love and serve?

Where are the people and places of peace? (People of peace - people who welcome you, listen to you, and are willing to serve you)

Who are the people to invite and connect?

How can you be good news to people?

What does good news look like to these people?

B. Individual Exercise (do it on your own)

Please write down the answers:

What is God's vision for you? (This could be joining someone else's vision)

Is it (formally) written down somewhere?

How is this vision revealed to you? Via Revelation, Holy Discontent or Hearts Desire? (or a combination) Did you see any confirmation of this?

Are there any words/pictures/ sense you've received (yourself or from others) that might be from God?

Do people around you, that could be your community/ church, know your vision? If yes, who? If not, why not?

What will be your next step to clarify/strengthen your vision?

- To whom are you accountable for this?

C. Shared Vision (Together with Spouse or Co-Leader)

Please write down the answers:

- What is the desire in your heart for your (extended) family?

- What are the qualities you would like to see for you as a (extended) family in your relationship with God?

- What do you want your (extended) family to look like on a weekly basis? E.g. prayers, food, fun.

- What are the things you would like to be known for by other people?

- What do you want to see multiplied and how are you going to do that?

D. UP, IN & OUT

Re-write your vision in UP, IN & OUT. It all starts in our own life. If we have vision for the world around us, how do we reflect what we would like to see in others? This is the question of integrity, how do we walk the talk in our personal life. What does the vision look like in daily life for you and your family? (leading by example)

YOU NEED TO KNOW THE 'WHY'

It's good to have a vision so that you know what you are working towards. However it doesn't say how you're going to achieve it, nor why you're doing what you're doing. Simon Sinek says that it is important to know your 'why.' Why do you get up in the morning? Why does your organization exist? Your 'why' is the purpose, cause or belief that inspires you to do what you do. When you think, act and communicate starting with 'why,' you can inspire others.

Although Sinek advises business organizations we think it is important for us as well to know our why. Too often we communicate what we are doing or what we would like to see happen, but we forget to mention our main motivation.

Besides the 'why' there is the 'how' and the 'what'. The 'how' is about the means by which are you going to do it. It is about your values and principles. It will help you to keep your co-workers accountable to these values. And finally the 'what' is the concrete living out of that vision and those values. Sinek puts these three in a diagram which he calls the 'Golden circle.' As you can see it starts with 'why' in the center, followed by 'how,' and then 'what' on the outside.

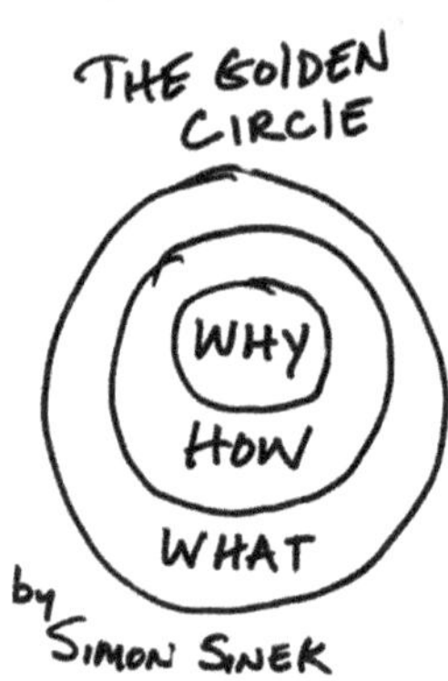

Helpful Guidelines for Writing your Vision

The following exercise can help you to write and communicate your vision.

Exercise

- Explain WHY you do what you do in two sentences at most. Start with: "I believe .... so that ...." and try to have a Covenant part as well as a Kingdom part. Example: I believe that every believer is part of God's family (Covenant) and therefore part of His mission so that we all are called to reach out to this world (Kingdom).

- Explain HOW do you do it. Mention two to five distinct characteristics or values about 'How' your community operates that makes you unique in the way you are going about realizing your vision. Try to use UP-IN-OUT. Start with: "We hold ourselves accountable to the following principles/values..." or "We are committed to..." Example: We are committed to grow a community where...
UP: We grow our intimacy with God and really learn in our ability in hearing His voice and depend on Him moment by moment. We to do this together in our community.
IN: With authentic relationships where it is safe to be yourself and you know you're accepted. We want to be known for our generosity and encouragement. We're excited to be on adventures together.
OUT: We want to carry this ordinary, integrated life out to the people around us in Hillsborough and we want to invite them into it.

- What do you do? Write down what you exactly do to realize this vision. Again try to use UP-IN-OUT: Start with: We .....
Example: We spend time together to pray, give thanks and worship God. We eat together and pray and prophesy for one another. We build relationships with our neighbors and invite them into our homes.

COMMUNICATION OF YOUR VISION

It is important to communicate vision wisely. This is not about having clever marketing strategies, but how to communicate our vision clearly.

Communication involves more than words. It involves:
- Logos - words and concepts,
- Ethos - behavior and character and
- Pathos - passion and sympathy

Clear communication is born of what you say, what you do and who you are. There must be integrity and alignment in order for your communication to be credible and persuasive. Some parents use the classic statement, "Do as I say". There's something inherently wrong about that. There is a kind of lack of integrity which undermines a person's ability to communicate their vision in a way that will infect others. They should be communicating: "Do as I do!" When we say things we don't do, we don't walk our talk and people won't believe us. In the end it is not about what people see, it is about our heart. "God examines every heart and sees through every motive" (1 Chronicles 28:9 MSG), but our desire has to be that we have integrity by communicating what we are doing ourselves. Basically that our communication is integrated in the way we live out our values and vision.

Sometimes we assume that people already know what we know. We do things intuitively without thinking about it. When we're communicating about mission and discipleship and inviting others into this, we need to be intentional to communicate what we already do automatically and find 'normal'. Don't assume that others understand and know things you've learned in the last year(s). It is important to walk our talk, but also to talk our walk!

So it is all about: integrity, integration, and being intentional!

CHAPTER 16

CALLING

What do we mean by calling? Our first or primary calling is to be in a Covenant relationship with God. As we've seen in the Chapter about Covenant and Kingdom (Chapter 2) this relationship gives us our identity. God is inviting us to be in relationship with Him by becoming a follower of Jesus. From this relationship with Him, we discover what He is calling us to do in the Kingdom. What our Kingdom responsibilities are.

Paul wrote in Ephesians 4:1-2 the following: "As a prisoner for the Lord, then, I urge you to live a life worthy of the calling you have received. Be completely humble and gentle; be patient, bearing with one another in love."

GUIDANCE OF GOD

Once we are followers of Jesus and in a relationship with the Father it's important to start with listening where to God is calling us. Graham Cooke says: "Guidance is the by-product of abiding in a right relationship with God. As we abide, we become sensitive to His heart."[2] So it all starts with God. When we live in covenant with God then we can trust that He is leading us to things He likes us to do. We don't have to work on our own to get things done and right, He is preparing us.
"And I tell you that you are Peter and on this rock I will build my church." (Matthew 16:18)
"Unless the Lord builds the house, the builders labor in vain." (Psalm 127:1)

As we look at Jesus as our great example, He only does the things he sees the Father doing. "I'm telling you this straight. The Son can't independently do a thing, only what He sees the Father doing. What the Father does, the Son does. The Father loves the Son and includes him in everything He is doing." (John 5:19 MSG). We, as children of the Father, are involved in the work He is already doing in this world! He is preparing us and the people and places around us!

God Doesn't Call the Equipped, But Equips the Called

We need to accept that God can call us to something we aren't yet. In the Bible we read several times that God qualified the unqualified. Where we think that someone isn't the right person God thinks differently. God starts with character.

Please find below some biblical examples (Moses, Jeremiah, David, the Disciples and Saul/Paul). God will equip them for their calling. They didn't find themselves equipped for the things asked them to do. Like we they looked at experience and skills, while God is looking at their hearts and how they are want to be shaped and transformed by Him.

Moses

"So now, go. I am sending you to Pharaoh to bring my people the Israelites out of Egypt." But Moses said to God, "Who am I that I should go to Pharaoh and bring the Israelites out of Egypt?" And God said, "I will be with you. And this will be the sign to you that it is I who have sent you: When you have brought the people out of Egypt, you will worship God on this mountain." (Exodus 3:10-12)

Jeremiah

"The word of the Lord came to me, saying, "Before I formed you in the womb I knew you, before you were born I set you apart; I appointed you as a prophet to the nations." "Alas, Sovereign Lord," I said, "I do not know how to speak; I am too young." But the Lord said to me, "Do not say, 'I am too young.' You must go to everyone I send you to and say whatever I command you. Do not be afraid of them, for I am with you and will rescue you," declares the Lord. Then the Lord reached out his

---

2   http://brilliantperspectives.com/god-always-says-yes/

hand and touched my mouth and said to me, "I have put my words in your mouth. See, today I appoint you over nations and kingdoms to uproot and tear down, to destroy and overthrow, to build and to plant." (Jeremiah 1:4-10)

David

"The Lord said to Samuel, "How long will you mourn for Saul, since I have rejected him as king over Israel? Fill your horn with oil and be on your way; I am sending you to Jesse of Bethlehem. I have chosen one of his sons to be king."

"When they arrived, Samuel saw Eliab and thought, "Surely the Lord's anointed stands here before the Lord." But the Lord said to Samuel, "Do not consider his appearance or his height, for I have rejected him. The Lord does not look at the things people look at. People look at the outward appearance, but the Lord looks at the heart." (1 Samuel 16:1, 6-7)

Disciples

"Afterward Jesus appeared in a different form to two of them while they were walking in the country. These returned and reported it to the rest; but they did not believe them either. Later Jesus appeared to the Eleven as they were eating; he rebuked them for their lack of faith and their stubborn refusal to believe those who had seen him after he had risen. He said to them, "Go into all the world and preach the gospel to all creation." (Mark 16:12-15). Even after spending 3 years with Jesus they still had a little faith and refuse to believe other believers who testified about Jesus' resurrection.

Saul/Paul (When Saul Was Called He Was Persecuting the Church)

"Meanwhile, Saul was still breathing out murderous threats against the Lord's disciples. As he neared Damascus on his journey, suddenly a light from heaven flashed around him. He fell to the ground and heard a voice say to him, "Saul, Saul, why do you persecute me?"

"Who are you, Lord?" Saul asked. "I am Jesus, whom you are persecuting," he replied. "Now get up and go into the city, and you will be told what you must do." (Acts 9:1, 3-6).

God calls you to give you the opportunity to do what you are created for. We need to prepare our hearts and attitude to step into the things He is calling us to do.

PART OF SOMETHING BIGGER

We can experience an individual calling, but God doesn't want us to operate as 'lone rangers'. We need to realize that we are part of something bigger. That's the way the body of Christ works. You can be called to act like a hand or foot, but you are part of the body, which means you have to work together.

Neil Cole emphasises this: "We need to fight against individualism in the body of Chris and keep united in the Spirit. This doesn't mean that we all have the same things God is calling us to do, but we always need to think how we can build the body of Christ together. We are called to unity, but there is a lot of diversity." We need to think how our calling is related to the body of Christ and also how we can build it. We are all called to unity, which requires a common commitment to humility.[3]

"Be completely humble and gentle; be patient, bearing with one another in love. Make every effort to keep the unity of the Spirit through the bond of peace." (Ephesians 4:2-3)

CONNECTION BETWEEN VISION, CALLING, FIVEFOLD AND IDENTITY

The easiest way of explaining the connection between vision, calling, fivefold and identity is via this picture.

---

3 Neil Cole, *Primal Fire.* Loc 1426

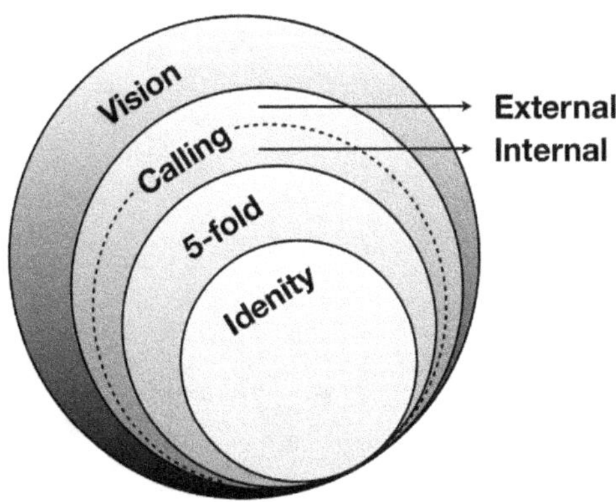

Some people prefer to start at the center with identity and others with vision. Calling is divided in two sections:

- Internal calling is the calling which God has called you to be (Covenant)
- External calling is the calling which God has called you to do (Kingdom)

Exercise:

*Fill out the Fivefold survey, which you can find
online: http://fivefoldsurvey.com
Make notes on what you learned:*

CHAPTER 17

UNDERLYING MOTIVATION

When we are following Jesus we want the things we do to be God-inspired and not a product of any self-focused desires, whether conscious or unconscious. Often, we can be influenced by negative or positive experiences of the past. We want to take some time to look at the underlying influences that may lead us to make decisions. Some of these may be positive or neutral but some can be faulty motivations. It may seem negative to search out these wrong motives, but often they point to positive things about our destiny and calling that need to be reclaimed. Often places of weaknesses are exactly where God wants to speak His identity and strength.

"But he said to me, "My grace is sufficient for you, for my power is made perfect in weakness." Therefore I will boast all the more gladly about my weaknesses, so that Christ's power may rest on me." (2 Corinthians: 12:9)

Not only can our past experiences influencing our motives, it also can limit our expectations. Why should it work now, when it didn't in the past?

Successively, we'll take a look at both positive and negative experiences.

POSITIVE EXPERIENCES

We could start a missional community or a ministry out of a positive experience like:

- Inspired by someone - here we need to ask if it is their calling or our calling?
- Influenced by culture - we can be drawn to start or to invite others into something because this reflects the culture we have been influenced by in the past. For us this was the missional discipleship culture in Sheffield.
- (Personal) successes from the past.

NEGATIVE OR HARD EXPERIENCES

We can start something because of what has happened to us such as:

- Rejection by people (the individuals or leadership of a church or organization).
- Someone did something to you.
- Someone failed to do something - disappointment.
- Wounded by family.
- Failures in the past (our own or others).
- Lack or absence of something.

We need to be sure that we have forgiven and have received healing or a kind of restoration process before we start to build something that "is the opposite of that."

Personal Examples: Negative or Hard Experience
Coming out of a legalistic background where Mark never had the Gospel presented clearly has given him a passion to make the Gospel easily accessible to all. This is the reason he is driven by evangelism, although he is not an evangelist.

Restoration: "I asked myself the question: how come the church I was brought up in, was so weak in presenting the Gospel and reaching out to non-believers? To answer this question I needed to look to the history of our church. The history of the Dutch Reformed churches is one of church splits. At some point in history we had 13 different Reformed churches. Back in these days it was really important that we as a church had the 'right doctrine' (interpretation of the Bible). So the main focus was on 'defending' our doctrinal tradition instead of sharing our beliefs with non-believers. A positive side of our church was that there was respect for God and His word."

Working as a church leader and inspired by missional communities, Mark started to implement these principles. He killed the small groups and then tried to start a missional community with the wrong people, which wasn't helpful. This experience could have put him off missional community forever. Instead it led him to learn by immersion. Mark: "I had to admit that I didn't know how to do it and that only reading the information wasn't sufficient enough. I realized I needed help to know how to start a missional community, but more than that how to start living missionally and in community."

Sharon has lived with many types of people. "Living with children was a real challenge, but I will not let that be a barrier to living with a family again if that is what God is calling me to. I realized that it was costly, but I still believe that a missional lifestyle and community can be for everyone, including families. What was really hard and stretched me, especially at the beginning, has trained me. Now I feel confident to relate to and disciple children and teenagers in the context of community. I have wonderful examples in my life now of the fruits of sacrificing for the next generation. I look at what God is doing in the lives of those children and am full of joy at the people they are becoming."

Examples: Positive Experience

Sharon: Influenced by culture. "The church I grew up in was very community orientated and we often had people living with us. There were two occasions when we had whole families living with us. It was just a normal part of our lives. When I first went to college it was the most natural thing in the world for me to share meals and create a sense of household with the people I lived near. It was in this context that I experienced my first real mission. Sharing my faith with those with whom I was sharing life. When I arrived in Sheffield after my college years I asked people to live with me intentionally for mission and we saw a wonderful time of fruitfulness. As a result I have invested myself in community ever since. This is a good thing, but I do not need to be limited by my first experiences of living in communities which was with single people. It does not always have to be the same: community houses can be made up of single people families, married people, and

any mixture of the above. Community does not always mean living under the same roof. It can be across a number of households intentionally integrating their weekly rhythms. Basically there are many different ways of living as a community!"

Mark: "At Crossroads Amsterdam I experienced a positive and encouraging American culture with focus on community (small groups) and personal development. There I learned about having a vision and discovered my fivefold role, which made a lot of sense. Suddenly the pieces of the puzzle came together. This helped me a lot in my journey of stepping out in faith. Members of the church were encouraged to develop themselves."

Mark: "My experience in Sheffield with missional discipleship has influenced my vision on how we live our lives right now. With the experience we now have with communities and discipleship I can't imagine living in a different way anymore. I'm convinced that this is a good context for learning how we can live a missional life and at the same time disciple people well."

Questions:

As we have talked about these issues, are there memories that have come to mind that you need to process, positive or negative? If there are, how and when will you begin to engage with these?

What experiences may have influenced your decision to start to living missionally, or to live as part of a missional community?

Are you doing this (living missional or in a missional community) as a calling or is it a reaction to something?

Do you need to forgive anyone to be free to move forward?

Do you think your past experiences are limiting you in your calling?

I

CHAPTER 18

THE FIVEFOLD GIFTS OF EPHESIANS 4

As you probably know there are a few Bible verses which talk about gifts in the church. Although these verses look the same, they aren't. There is a distinction between spiritual gifts (Romans 12:6-7, 1 Corinthians 12:1-11 and 1 Peter 4:9-11) and roles within the church (Ephesians 4:1-13).

The role is the job or function. The gifts are supernatural tools to use within that role. To help us in differentiating the gifts from a specific role, it's important to look at the context in which each passage was written.[4]

The letters to the Romans and Corinthians are written to specific churches with specific problems. When Paul addresses spiritual gifts in Corinth it is about the worship services and how the Holy Spirit works amongt his people. He will activiate gifts and empower them for the particular task. So these gifts aren't permanent roles. The gifts (wisdom, knowledge, faith, miraculous powers, prophecy, distinguishing between spirits, speaking in different kinds of tongues, interpretation of tongues) are also called *manifestational gifts*. In Romans Paul wrote about the division within the church. It's not working as a united body. Therefore he gives instructions about sacrifice and service. He calls us to serve one another with the gift God has given. These gifts (prophesy, serving, teaching, encourage, giving, lead, showing mercy) are also called *motivational gifts*.

The letter to the Ephesians was not written to just one church for a special moment in time, but for all the churches in Asia Minor. It outlines foundational teachings about how a church should function. Paul shares what the roles of all believers are to be within the church.[5]

SPIRITUAL GIFTS AND FRUIT OF THE SPIRIT

There is a difference between spiritual gifts and fruit. Gifts are the Spirit's manifestation through a person, but fruit is the 'result' of one's spiritual character. Spirituality cannot be measured by gifts, but by fruit (Galatians 5:22-24). Love is the predominate feature of spirituality (1 Corinthians 13:13), without which, charismatic gifts cannot function effectively (1 Corinthians 13:1-2). Paul said the church should have a desire for spiritual gifts, but first and foremost it should pursue love. "Follow the way of love and eagerly desire gifts of the Spirit, especially prophecy." (1 Corinthians 14:1).

EPHESIANS 4

It is our belief that the roles of apostle, prophet, evangelist, shepherd (pastor) and teacher, were given to the church to bring the full expression of Christ's beauty and glory in the world. It is only when all these gifts are released to function naturally in the body and they mature to the point of equipping others that the church will fully reflect Jesus - in all His beauty - to the world.[6]

Jesus was perfect and had all the gifts He needed, despite the fact He called his disciples to serve with him. Each body of Christ has received together all the gifts needed, but these are not reflected in one person. To operate as a body of Christ it's helpful to know what our roles are, so that we learn what our strengths but also our weaknesses are. This helps us to:

- See what our areas of growth are
- Recognize how others can support us
- Learn how we can function well as the body of Christ together

---

4   Mike Breen, *Buidling a Discipling Culture*, p135-136

5   Mike Breen, *Buidling a Discipling Culture*, p136

6   Neil Cole, *Primal Fire*, Loc. 314, 330

Lets take a closer look at these roles or gifts:
"But to each one of us grace has been given as Christ apportioned it... So Christ himself gave the apostles, the prophets, the evangelists, the pastors and teachers, to equip his people for works of service, so that the body of Christ may be built up until we all reach unity in the faith and in the knowledge of the Son of God and become mature, attaining to the whole measure of the fullness of Christ." (Ephesians 4:7, 11-13)

In Ephesians 4:7 Paul says "each one of us" has been given the grace. Therefore we believe that these gifts are not only for the leaders or 'special people' of a church or organization, but that everyone has been given the gift of either, apostle, prophet, evangelist, pastor or teacher. We are aware this may require a change in thinking for some pastors and leaders and could be threatening to some of them. But the great news is that the fivefold gifts are all about releasing members of the body to function at their full potential![7] Every Christian has a ministry which is meant to flow out of our role and gifting. For us it is important to find out our personal calling so that we can equip the body to function like Christ and to follow his direction.

Maybe you already know your role, or you're already on this journey, and that's great. If not, this could be the start of a journey to find out. We want to help people find out what their role is, how to grow in that role, and how the different roles of the Fivefold can work together. It is amazing that Christ has been given a powerful role to every disciple. We'd love to see everyone released into their God-given roles. This is the way God is equipping and growing the church!

Alan Hirsch uses the following description for the five roles or gifts:[8]

- Apostle/apostolic: Apostle means literally sent one. It is very much a pioneering function of the church, the capacity to extend Christianity as a healthy, integrated, innovative, reproducing movement, ever-expanding into new churches.
- Prophet/prophetic: is the function tasked with maintaining and abiding loyalty and faithfulness to God above all.
- Evangelist/evangelistic: involves the proclamation of the Good News that is at the core of the church's message.
- Shepherd/shepherding: is the function and calling responsible for maintaining and developing healthy community and enriching relationships.
- Teacher/teaching: is concerned with the mediation and appropriation of wisdom and understanding.

Start With Genuine Relationships

In his book *Primal Fire*, Neil Cole writes: "In our thirty years of experience, we have found that focusing on our own gifts and the strengths that we bring to the church does not produce unity at all. In fact, it's almost guaranteed to bring separation. Rather than starting with our gifted orientation, we must begin by establishing genuine relationships with one another. Surrendering our strength and glory for the benefit of others, which is really just love, is the foundation of unity. Our relationships must be more important than anyone's agenda or abilities."[9] Mutual submission is particularly necessary when addressing the APEST roles of Ephesians 4.

Be Aware of the Shadow Side

Cole continues: "Each one of the five gifts has an area of weakness that casts a shadow a part of the gift that is not always positive. This shadow is always easier for others to recognize than it is for the one who casts the shadow. Until we recognize our own weaknesses,

---

7   Mike Breen, *Building a Discipling Culture*, Loc. 1767

8   Alan Hirsch, *5Q, Reactivating the Original Intelligence and Capacity of the Body of Christ*

9   Neil Cole, *Primal Fire*. Loc 281

we will not achieve real unity. But when we come to recognize our own shadows, we begin to appreciate the other gifts more. The secret to forming a team of the various gifts is to focus, not on the strengths of each one, but rather on their weaknesses. Only then will we have the unity necessary to be a potent, diverse team."[10] Here you'll find some of these shadow sides of the different gifts:

Apostle: They can jump (around) from one idea to the next, unable to stay focused on one thing. Eventually, people stop following them

Prophet: They can talk about their perspective as though it was simply the truth. They move from church to church because they keep finding issues in each. They can easily become Lone Rangers.

Evangelist: They can devalue discipleship and transformation in favor of the excitement of getting new people involved. They focus on converts instead of making disciples.

Shepherd: In their care for individual people, they can lose track of the bigger picture of being on mission. Because they are so transformation-oriented they may resist momentum in the church because "we're not ready."

Teacher: In their hunt for clarity, they can offend people with their bluntness. Immature teachers lack empathy. In their desire to know the truth and make truth known, they may end up with a lot of head knowledge without practice.

Don't Forget the Giver

Thinking about our personal calling and the spiritual gifts we received it could cause self-focus or individualism, where it is all about ourselves. What is my calling, what is my role, what is my gifting? We can be so focused on what we're doing and our gifts that we forget the Giver himself! [11]

Your Role/Gift is Not Your Identity

Your identity comes from the fact that you are a son or daughter of God through Jesus. That gives you your identity. From that identity you can cooperate with God in the way how He has wired you.

BASE AND PHASE

Although we're all called to be a witness, hear God's voice, to be hospitable, etc. the role we do most naturally is what is called a 'Base Ministry'.[12] It's more or less the way God has wired us. But God can also teach us to learn to function in the other roles during certain periods, called 'Phase Ministry'. In these seasons we can experience the other gifts and it will help us to serve the body of Christ. You will learn the basics, you don't need to excel in all five. Our experience is that there are often two gifts of the Fivefold which are quite natural, and one of them is our base ministry. It is important to realize that we can't be everything and that we need each other!

Since every person is unique (personality profile, different backgrounds, and different contexts), people with the same base ministry may look different!

Personal Example

Jacolien: a few years ago I started to think about my personal calling and found out that the prophetic gifting really resonated with me. Being around prophetic people and learning from them was really helpful to find out more about the prophetic. I've learned that this is the role I go back to when I'm feeling dry. There were phases in my life when I've pastored people as a counselor and social worker. I now know that this was a phase ministry, because that took quite a lot of energy, but I learned a lot during that time and am very grateful for that. The apostolic role also feels quite natural for me because I like to set up new things. But being around apostolic people has shown it is more natural for

---

10   Neil Cole, *Primal Fire.* Loc 281

11   Neil Cole, *Primal Fire.* Loc 542

12   Mike Breen, *Building a Discipling Culture.* p122

me to speak truth and try to discern what God is saying, than lead into new territory.

Personal Example

Mark: I am an apostle and teacher as a Base Ministry. I'm always looking for new ways, how we can improve things, and I like change. At the same time I'd like to hand over my knowledge and experience. I'm looking for other people to train and equip.
Shepherd was a Phase Ministry fo rme. When I was a pastor I needed to set up pastoral care teams. I taught a course and started to have conversations with people. I learned a basic set of skills and I'm confident enough that I can help people to process. Currently I'm exploring and growing in Prophecy as a Phase Ministry.

IMPORTANCE OF MATURITY AND EQUIPPING

Knowing our Base role doesn't mean we don't have the responsibility to serve in the other areas of the Fivefold! We are all called to be a witness, to hear God's voice, to care for one another, to step out in faith, and to explain the word to others. Like every child, we all need to read, to write, and learn the basic life skills to function in this world. Every Christian needs to have a basic set of skills and for everyone of us that is a growing process. It's not only about growing in our strength but knowing our weaknesses and becoming more mature in these areas. It is important to remember that our gifting won't take us where our character can't keep us.

Neil Cole emphasises the importance of disciple-making when he writes: "The key is to get each individual part working correctly for the health of the whole body. If we want the church to be healthy, we must elevate our standard of disciple-making. Better sermons, bigger buildings, booming sound systems, and blasting bands are not what make a healthy church. The church is only as strong as its disciples. Every individual part must contribute to the whole. Each is measured ("proper working") against Christ and must always be following Him if the body is ever to express the fullness of Christ to the world."[13]

"Every follower of Jesus has been gifted by God to serve and build up Christ's body. We've all been given gifts, and some will become gifts as they mature in the APEST roles. Someone who has matured to the place where he or she is a spiritual parent to others is what an equipping gift is about". [14]

EXPLORERS AND DEVELOPERS

We've learned two different ways to categorize the fivefold gifts: Apostles, prophets, and evangelists can be described as the explorers, while pastors and teachers can be described as developers.[15]
Neil Cole prefers to speak about the 'Start & Go Team', which are the apostles and prophets, and the 'Stay & Grow Team' which are the evangelists, shepherds, and teachers.[16] The latter are the ESTablish Team who build on the foundation laid by the Apostles and Prophets.

Thinking about this, I came to see that many of the Explorers (or Start & Go Team) in existing churches have become frustrated and moved into parachurch organizations to do their ministry. There is a tension in churches between those who think things are changing too slowly, and those who think change is happening too fast. The fivefold framework brings clarity to these tensions. Explorers journey into the wilderness and stake out new ground beyond existing civilization. But after a short while, explorers will always move on to the next wilderness. If developers do not follow soon after the explorers, the new land will return to wilderness. So, planting healthy community in new places requires both

---

13   Neil Cole, *Primal Fire*, Loc 1607

14   Neil Cole, *Primal Fire*. Loc 1750

15   Mike Breen, *Building a Discipling Culture*. p127

16   Neil Cole, *Primal Fire*. Loc 2441

explorers and developers.

COMMUNITY

When building a community, it is really helpful to know and understand each other's base ministries - to recognize how we can function as a body, to be interdependent instead of individualistic. We get to know and learn to communicate our weaknesses, so we can be vulnerable and allow other people to help us build a culture of serving each other. Also we can train and equip others in our Base Ministry so we help the community in growing together to become more mature and be more like Jesus.

Question:
Proximity - how close are people? How much time do you spend together?

Questions:

What stood out for you in this Chapter?

What do you think is your base ministry?

If you don't know, how can you get more clarity?

When you know your base ministry: what do you need to learn to become more mature? What are the pitfalls? Where do you need other people? How do you equip others (from your base ministry)? What are the ministries of the people in your team? Of your community? How can you serve one another?

STEPPING STONE FIVE

FORMING A SPIRITUAL FAMILY

CHAPTER 19

FROM LEADERSHIP TO SPIRITUAL PARENTS

There are a lot of books written about leadership and also about Christian leadership. We'd love to keep it simple. The shortest, and we think, the most clear definition is from John Maxwell: "Leadership is influence."[1] In this definition you don't have to be in a formal position or role to be a leader. You don't need to have all the knowledge or be an explorer/apostle who is always pressing into the frontier and doing new things. We believe that every one can influence someone else and therefore every ordinary person can be a leader!

Leadership has a lot similarities with discipleship. Discipling others is serving, teaching, training, modelling, encouraging etc. and this is how we influence and lead others. Basically when you're discipling one person you are a leader. And because we believe in life-long learning we can be both a leader and a learner at the same time. We like to say: "We are shepherds from the back and sheep from the front."

SPIRITUAL INFLUENCE

In Mark 10.42-43 Jesus says to his disciples: "You know that those who are regarded as rulers of the Gentiles lord it over them, and their high officials exercise authority over them. Not so with you. Instead, whoever wants to become great among you must be your servant." So leadership is not about exercising authority, aspiring and striving for position and hierarchical leadership or, 'throwing your weight around' (Mark 10:42-43 MSG). Leadership should be nonhierarchical and far more based on personal responsibility and accountability. In *Primal Fire*, Neil Cole writes about the early church: "In the first century, as a new faith ignited and spread like wildfire across the world, leadership tended to be nonhierarchical, its authority derived from spiritual influence. As the movement unexpectedly and organically swept through the Roman Empire, it was a true expression of what missiologist Roland Allen calls "the spontaneous expansion of the church." But as soon as position, money, and power entered the mix, a politicizing of the bride of Christ seeped in, and her reliance on faith was diminished. No longer an organic movement that distributed the powerful presence of Christ to all, the church quickly became an institution that sucked all the life inward. The movement became a monument."[2]

When leadership is based on position instead of spiritual influence we often see a pyramid model as the leadership structure. This kind of structure gives less space for creating a culture of discipleship where people are listening to God themselves and taking responsibility to act on this and are being accountable, which we call low-control, high-accountability.

THE NEED FOR SPIRITUAL PARENTS

The culture of the church has moved to a place, where it is possible to manage a congregation of 100, 500 or even more than 1000 people. However managing people is often focused on maintaining systems and processes and is something different from influencing people to follow. A leader can lead by sharing vision, inspiring people, giving direction and telling them what to do, but we all know that you can't disciple that many people. If Jesus discipled twelve people, and one didn't work out so well, why do we think we can disciple hundreds?

What we need are leaders who are willing to open up their lives and start discipling people. Larry Kreider says: "God's intention is to produce spiritual parents who

---

1   John C. Maxwell, www.christianitytoday.com/pastors/2007/july-online-only/090905.html

2   *Primal Fire*, Loc 812-825

are willing to nurture spiritual children and help them grow into spiritual parents. This is the fulfilment of the Lord's promise to "turn the hearts of the fathers to the children and the hearts of the children to their fathers" (Malachi 4:6). The Lord is restoring harmony between mothers and fathers - both natural and spiritual - and their children, so that parents can freely impart their inheritance to the next generation."[3]

Discipleship is more like parenting children. Parents lead a family with children and this kind of leadership is quite different from a managerial style of leadership. It's interesting to read what Paul wrote to the Thessalonians: Just as a nursing mother cares for her children, so we cared for you. Because we loved you so much, we were delighted to share with you not only the gospel of God but our lives as well. For you know that we dealt with each of you as a father deals with his own children, encouraging, comforting and urging you to live lives worthy of God, who calls you into his kingdom and glory. (1 Thessalonians 2:7-8, 11-12)

There are many examples in the Bible. Moses discipled Joshua, or in other words was a spiritual father to him. Elijah was a spiritual father to Elisha, Elizabeth a spiritual mother to Mary and Paul a spiritual father to Timothy.

In 1 Corinthians 4:14,15 Paul wrote: "I am writing this not to shame you but to warn you as my dear children. Even if you had ten thousand guardians in Christ, you do not have many fathers, for in Christ Jesus I became your father through the gospel."

David Devenisch comes to the conclusion that, for Paul, the members of the Corinthian church were not just people who had responded to his teaching and therefore joined this new Christian organization, they were his spiritual children.[4]

Since the main focus of discipleship is raising 'spiritual' children, we need:

- Spiritual parents who can do this and
- A 'family-like unit' where it can take place.

Spiritual Parents: similar to a biological family we need spiritual parents. A good way to do that is by sharing responsibility. At least two people need to lead a household or community. Those two can be a married couple, but also two single people or in our case a couple and a single person.

Family-Like Unit: the New Testament calls this type of family 'oikos', which is a Greek word for 'households', which were essentially extended families who functioned together with a common purpose. In the early church discipleship and mission always centered around and flourished in the oikos.[5]

Questions:
Can you think of people who have been spiritual parents to you?
To whom are you opening your life and be accountable? Personally and in your role as a leader for others?
What is your most natural leadership style?
As a disciple, how easily are you led?
Are you a spiritual parent? Do you first need to grow as a son/daughter before you step into parenthood?
Where are you in this process?

---

3   Larry Kreider, *Cry for Spiritual Mothers and Fathers.* p25

4   D. Devenish, *Fathering Leaders, Motivating Mission.* p67

5   Mike Breen, *Leading Missional Communities.* p4

CHAPTER 20

PERSONAL AND SHARED VALUES

We find that most people make decisions according to a few 'core values,' but many have never taken the time to articulate just what those values are. In fact they may never have consciously identified the values that motivate them. We need to move back from unconscious competence to conscious competence.

Definition

According to Carlos Jeminez, values are the internal principles we hold dear, that guide our behavior to ensure we fulfill ourselves as individuals and live satisfied lives.[6]

Values are also:
- Our fundamental beliefs and they reflect our strongest feelings and convictions.
- Concerned with human needs and represent our ideals, dreams and aspirations.
- Not good in their own right. They can be godly or ungodly.

In the present, they help us choose what we will actually do In any given situation: For example, when using public transportation, some people give their seat to a pregnant woman and some don't, depending on their values. Give up seat: valuing politeness and consideration for others. Don't give up seat: valuing own comfort above politeness or valuing your own needs to be seated (e.g. if you are an elderly person, pregnant yourself etc.)

For the future they provide guidelines to enable us to formulate our goals and objectives, whether these are personal or collective.

Our values are important to us regardless of:
- The circumstances we find ourselves in - grandparents may value spending time with their grandchildren, but their children (parents of the grandchildren) moved to another town.
- Other people's opinions - we may value leisure, but be surrounded by people who do not see it as a worthy use of time.
- Our own behavior - we may value patience but lose our temper.

When we're guided by values, we act without expecting anything in return, except personal satisfaction and fulfilment.

Discuss:
Can you give an example of a value which is important to you? And can you relate it to one of the above categories?

---

6   http://significanceofvalues.com/definition/, *The Significance of Values in an Organization*, by C. Jimenez

HOW OUR VALUES HAVE BEEN FORMED

We start forming values in our childhood. We value those people that provide for our basic needs. Their behavior towards us becomes the main reference of what is valuable. Thus, our character and personality are molded through the attitudes and behavior of the people who raise us, whether they're our parents or other relatives. We learn to value the substance and the form of everything they say and do, and what they don't say and don't do.

Each gesture or comment affects how we learn to make choices. We also learn to differentiate between the theory and practice of values. The latter is what marks us the most. So the consistency and coherence of our parents' behavior is what strengthens our formation. If they practice what they preach, our personality will be stronger than if they don't.

Difficult to Change Values

Why is it so difficult to change our values? Because, unlike norms, values are convictions; they lead to behaviors we gladly decide to follow which produce satisfaction. We can follow norms against our will, but values have the support of our will. We have learned their importance due to the benefits they produce, individually and collectively.

Values are Foundational to Succes

Values are foundational. They have to match the goal or mission of the community or group because:
- They create the culture.
- They provide clear expectations and boundaries.
- They are like a compass that helps us behave consistently, regardless of the situation.
- They provide a template for decisions and plans.
- They have to be reflected in the actual behavior of the members of the group to be real and not simply a list of ideals.

People may express their values as ideas and concepts but what we appreciate is what they actually do. We can see peoples' values by their practices and the patterns they commit to in their lives.

CHRISTIAN VALUES
- When we become Christians we become children of God again.
- We must turn to our heavenly Father to provide our basic needs.
- His behavior towards us becomes the main reference for what is valuable.
- All our previous values need to be compared to the values He demonstrates to us.

Psalm 37:4 says: "Take delight in the Lord and he will give you your heart's desires." (NLT) If we do this we will begin to allow him to bring our internal motivations, convictions, and deeply held values into line with his own. We are blessed if we have people alongside us who are demonstrating these values to us.

"A good person produces good things from the treasury of a good heart, and an evil person produces evil things from the treasury of an evil heart." - Matthew 12:35 (NLT)

What Disciples and Disciplers Need to Do:
- Know our Father's values - through searching his Word and listening to the testimony of his people.
- Embrace our Father's values - through thanksgiving, worship, personal repentance, forgiveness for self and others and by allowing God's healing to restore our hearts with his love.
- As we make this journey we will discover our God-given values.
- Live our lives based on the values he has implanted in our hearts and make them visible to others through our behavior, practices and patterns.
- Articulate these values and call others to them.
- Minister these values to those we lead, e.g. pray with them for revelation and healing so they can begin to embrace them for themselves and in turn demonstrate them to others.

As we live life on life with those we are discipling they will learn and receive our godly values as we convey them through the example of our daily attitudes and behaviors.

Values are only passed on through the example of our daily attitudes and behaviors. They can seldom be formed by explaining them or through a list of what is considered correct or incorrect. Memorizing their theoretical meaning does not guarantee their implementation. To convey godly values we must first possess them, counting them a precious part of what matters to us deeply.

Dennis Rainey wrote: "If you want to leave a godly legacy, you first must determine what you believe in—what is most important to you. And then you need to evaluate how well you are living according to those values, because your (spiritual) children will learn from your actions and lifestyle more than your words. For example, if one of your core values is, My family comes before my job, and they see you consistently working so many hours that you rarely have time to spend with them, they'll conclude that your real core value is, My work is more important than my family".[7]

To find out God's values - look at the life of Jesus, the story of Scripture, the admonitions of the letters, your own testimony, and the stories of God's work in others.

Personal Examples - Values Worked Out in Community

Sharon, Generosity - honoring people freely, speaking out words of affirmation even when it feels costly, sharing time together (being followed around the house by young interns asking questions!), money (paying for a flight or a night out or giving money for prescription or giving new shoes, etc.), possessions (sharing car, coffee machine, knowledge, friendships etc).

Mark, Teamwork & Adventure - living a missional lifestyle isn't something to do on your own. I'd love to see it as going on an adventure together like a band of brothers and sisters. Exploring new things, standing side by side and complementing each other.

Jacolien - Authenticity - to be transparent (sharing what's going on, what was and is difficult), to be vulnerable (to ask for prayer when I'm not feeling great), to be honest (saying what I think when it's hard for people to say or hear, not having 'hidden' agenda's in relationships), to have integrity (doing what I'm saying and living out the vision and values which are important to me), and trying not to boast and to listen to others so that's not all about me.

Questions:
What stood out for you in this Chapter?
Can you think of one core value which is important to you?
What is on God's heart which contradicts our values or is not represented in what we hold dear?
Will we choose to embrace this value? If so what will our steps be?

---

7   Dennis Rainey, https://www.idisciple.org/post/determining-your-core-values

Exercise [8]

Part One - Personal Core Values: Become Conscious of Your Values (complete Part One individually)
Take some time on your own (!) to:

- Think about what gives you joy. When something happens or we think about something and we experience joy it is often because one of our values is being demonstrated and played out.
- Think about times when are you feeling uncomfortable or what gives you pain, what makes you angry? This may indicate that one of your values was violated.
- Review where you invested your energy in recent years? Why did you do it? What is the value that led you to invest in this way?
- Write down the values related to the answers you gave for questions 1-3. A helpful tool can be the list of 418 values (see Appendix 2).
- Try to categorize them in UP-IN-OUT (relationship with God, relationships with other Christians and relationships with non-Christians)

From this list, designate your Top 6 Core Values list:

	UP		IN		OUT
1		3		5	
2		4		6	

Part Two - Shared Values: Developing a Unified List (interact as spiritual parents)
Share your answers from Part One with your spouse/the other leader/spiritual parent. In what areas do you agree and disagree with each other's conclusions? How are you different? Talk about the ways you need one another for balance.

Now develop a unified Top 6 Core Values list. Again categorised by UP-IN-OUT.
Close in prayer together, confessing any failures in this area and asking God to enable you to live according to your Core Values. Be thankful for diversity and complementarity.

Part Three - Plan: Developing a Plan for Installing Core Values
Incarnating the values. Which rhythms do you have in place to model this values? What do you need to change to model these 6 values to your community? What ideas do you have for helping your community to live by these core values? What words/vocabulary do you want to use to start communicating the values?

6 Months Goals

Value	Goal	Stop		Start		Responsible	Completed by
		Internal	External	Internal	External		

---

8   Based on Dennis Rainey's worksheet to determine your core beliefs and values

Example of Values - Missional Community 'INSIDE OUT,' Sheffield UK

Values UP

1. Guidance - Hearing His voice - ambition - vs hearing your own voice
2. Intimacy - Live in intimate relationship - approval - affirmation of God instead of people
3. Dependability - Live in His presence depending on Him moment by moment - appetite, feeling the need for provision

Values IN

1. Integrity & Authenticity - safety - depth
2. Teamwork & Adventure - Band of brothers/sisters, being on an adventure together
3. Generosity - Environment of generosity

Values OUT

1. (Missional) Zeal - Living a missional lifestyle
2. Transparency. Accessibility. Authenticity. Inclusive. Ordinary life.

Our Vision

We are committed to grow a community where:

UP: We grow our intimacy with God and really learn to hear His voice and depend on Him, moment by moment. We to do this together in our community.

IN: We build authentic relationships where it is safe to be yourself and you know you're accepted. We want to be known for our generosity and encouragement. We're excited to be on adventures together.

OUT: We want to carry this ordinary, integrated life out to the people around us in Hillsborough and we want to invite them into it. (See also Chapter 15 about Vision and Communication)

CHAPTER 21

CALLING PEOPLE

This chapter is about inviting people to join you on mission. That can be co-leaders, co-spiritual parents, or followers who will become family members.

THE RIGHT REASON

When you invite people, to join you, the most important thing is that you invite them for the right reason. The main reason should be: to help make disciples who make disciples. It is really important to be on the same page. This doesn't mean that someone needs to know everything about discipleship and has a lot of experience with it (maybe less experience is better!).

Investing in people costs time, energy and resources. The leadership style Jesus showed us was based on a process that takes time and vulnerability. Time to lead someone through the different phases and vulnerability to open your life to be in community and really get to know each other (even our 'bad hair' days).

We've seen some leaders, including ourselves (!), invite others to join them to complete a task and they begin by giving information. As soon as the knowledge is shared, they send people out to do the job. This is a task-focused approach which doesn't necessarily include a shared life and building intentional community. This is not sustainable.

When you decide you are going to take a more relational approach by inviting others to join you, it's important that we don't only look for people with the right competence. It's good to invite people with competencies in specific areas, but look for other aspects as well and do not decide too quickly.

HELPFUL CRITERIA

Here is a list of criteria which can help you in the process of inviting the right people:

1. Character - Personally we think this is the most important one. We look for specific character traits in those we invite. You want people who are humble, vulnerable, transparant, willing to adopt a lifestyle of learning and serving, and ready to submit themselves to your (God-given) vision.

2. Chemistry - When you're going to live and work closely together then it's important to find people that you 'click' with. Sometimes we overlook this, but it is very helpful when we actually like each other!

3. Calling - Look for people with a similar calling, or people who have another calling but want to follow you for a specific period. If they have another calling then you need to discuss the expectations and the timeframe in which they will join you. It is very helpful to understand to their base ministry in the Fivefold roles. Are they willing to grow in the other Fivefold roles (phase ministry)? How does this fit with your own Fivefold role? For example, if you both are apostles, how will you work with each other? Do both apostles have enough space to explore new territory? Be aware that, in time, apostles need to be released.
You can also ask if there is a gifting gap in the team. Sometimes you need to call someone with a specific Fivefold role to fill in what is missing in your team, although that doesn't mean you necessarily have to include all the Fivefold roles on your team.

4. Capacity - Does the person have time and space in his/her life to do what you expect them to do? Is this the right season? From our own experience we've seen quite a few times that it wasn't the right time for people to join the team because of personal/family circumstances.

5. Competence - Calling people only because of their skills is a fatal mistake. We believe that 'God doesn't call the equipped, He equips the called.' But some level of competence is necessary. The questions you can ask are: what are the minimum set of skills someone needs to serve on your team? Do the people you're calling need a proper training process and if so, what does that look like? Be aware that training can't change someone's personality.

6. Culture - You are inviting people into something that could be counter-cultural for them. This culture of missional discipleship is different from many church cultures. If you're part of this missional movement for a while, be aware that you've already made some major paradigm shifts, which the people you want to invite probably haven't made yet. For example, an emphasis on discipleship could mean the priority is not organizing events for large groups of people, but building relationships with people who are open to you. This process is much slower. When you're calling people it is important to talk with them about your core values which reflect the (discipleship) culture you want to create.

When the call is to move to another country, naturally there is a literal change of culture and the challenges that come with that. It is good to talk about that with the people involved and consider what kind of impact this could have. How flexible are they and how will they stay in contact with people in their home country? These things need to be discussed early on in the process.

7. Counting the Cost - It is important to consider a person's willingness to (partly) give up control, privileges, privacy and comfort. Are they willing to to be pruned? If someone needs to move to a different place, are they willing to leave family and friends behind? It is important to be specific about these sacrifices and talk about what it means in their daily lives. People often don't realize what the costs are to lay their lives down in particular areas. It is better to realize this beforehand than afterwards. Living on a mission will not always be easy. Jesus never promised us the road will be smooth, but God will give us grace when we're willing to take up our cross and follow his calling.

8. Couples and Children - When someone is married (or engaged) then you always need to include the partner in the process. Have conversations with both of them. If the couple has children then the kids need to be part of it as well. Basically what you're looking for is a 'full-family-commitment'.

9. Cost of Living - They need to consider how they will support themselves financially.

Other Topics to Think About

Calling Peers - When you're calling a peer who is going to co-lead with you be aware that they probably also need to be discipled on specific topics. Are they willing to be part of a discipling process? (E.g. in our case living with Sharon who had more experience in missional community and evangelism).

Personality - Moving from annoyance to appreciation. It's is so good to get to know ourselves and each other's personalities. We've learned that when we become personally more self-aware, we get insight in our own pitfalls (weaknesses) and learn that we need each other. Alongside that, we are more able to appreciate learning from each other's strengths. Then we are going from annoyance to appreciation. We've found the Myers Briggs personality inventory a great instrument for this.

When There is Already a Team - As leaders/spiritual parents of an existing community it is important to check with other leaders and hear their thoughts about a new person you are considering for the team. We don't think you need to vote, but if there are hesitations you need to take this seriously. The question is do they need to be lay down these feelings/thoughts (counting the cost) or is it better not to invite that person.

DECISION-MAKING PROCESS

As you can see there are some things to think about before you invite someone. It can be overwhelming and maybe you think who can check all these boxes? Probably nobody. What we've learned is to take time before choosing team members utilizing an intentional decision-making process. It's better to spend time at the beginning than facing issues later.

Personal Example:
Mark and Jacolien: We used a decision-making process to form a church-planting team with another couple. After a few months of getting to know each other and sharing vision, they decided that it wasn't the right season for them as a family to work with us.
We used a decision-making process to start a missional household in Sheffield. We went through a four-month process with a total of four people. In the end three out of the four people ended up moving in with us.

Practical Insights
Some practical insights on a decision-making process:
- Take your time. 3-6 months may look look like a very long time, but honestly, it isn't.
- Set an end date by when you plan to make a decision.
- Be accountable to that plan.
- Spend time with one another for meals, prayer, listening to God, and sharing expectations.
- If possible start to live UP-IN-OUT rhythms together, this gives you a flavor of what it could look like in the future.
- If you don't live in the same city, plan days and/or weekends to spend time together. When you can't meet physically, use Zoom or Skype.
- Use low control, high accountability - give people the freedom to say no.

STEPPING STONE SIX

MULTIPLYING MISSIONAL LIFE

CHAPTER 22

SOWING, GROWING AND REAPING

God can break through in power, but often He expects us to be co-workers with Him in the process of evangelism.[1] 1 Corinthians 3:9: "For we are co-workers in God's service; you are God's field, God's building."

I (Mark) don't have a 'green thumb' but I do like the metaphor used in the Bible for the faith process. We read about sowing, watering, growing and reaping. Although the Bible tells us the growth process is a mystery, this process can be helpful to us.

SOWING

In the Gospel of Mark we find this parable of Jesus: "Listen! A farmer went out to sow his seed. As he was scattering the seed, some fell along the path, and the birds came and ate it up. Some fell on rocky places, where it did not have much soil. It sprang up quickly, because the soil was shallow. But when the sun came up, the plants were scorched, and they withered because they had no root. Other seed fell among thorns, which grew up and choked the plants, so that they did not bear grain. Still other seed fell on good soil. It came up, grew and produced a crop, multiplying thirty, sixty, or even a hundred times." (Mark 4:3-8)

We can sow everywhere and anytime. When we have chance encounters with people (passing relationships) we can take the risk of using more spiritual content and language (prayer and prophecy), because there is and probably won't be an ongoing relationship. With our ongoing relationships like family, friends, neighbors, and colleagues (permanent relationships) you'll probably

be a little bit more careful when you sow the Word and how you sow. With them we can use a more gradual approach by inviting them for a meal, yearly celebrations like, Halloween, Christmas, Easter, and sports events. Or we may just invite people to hang out together.

The Inverted Triangle

This diagram is used by Laurence Singlehurst.[2] It explains the process of bringing people through a journey of sowing, reaping and keeping. Bob & Mary Hopkins added an extra section (S3) to the original diagram and look at this process as 'pools for fishing':[3]

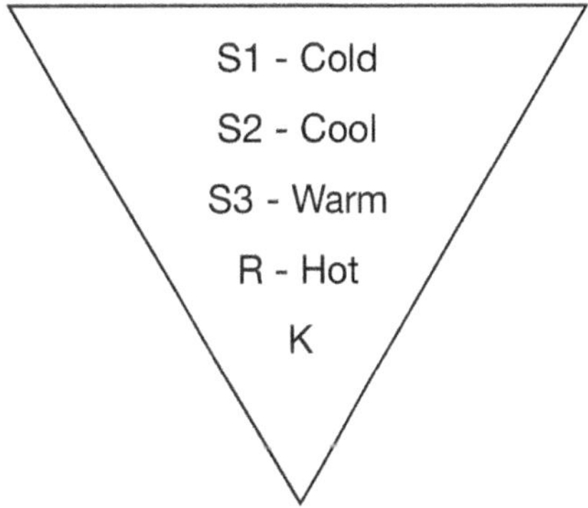

- Sowing 1 (S1) is the Cold Pool where there is no overt Gospel content. We'll invite people in this cool pool just to hang out and have fun so that we can get to know one another, e.g. movie nights, game nights, barbecues, watching sports, etc. This is how we begin to look for People of Peace.
- Sowing 2 (S2) is the Cool Pool with some Gospel content, e.g. meals with thanksgiving, highs and lows, prayers for blessing with no expectation of

---

1 *Evangelism Strategies*, Hopkins Ch16

2 L. Singlehurst, *Sowing Reaping Keeping: People-Sensitive Evangelism.* ebook location 1674

3 *Evangelism Strategies*, Hopkins.

spiritual participation, a Thanksgiving meal with opportunity to write blessings and prayers, a Christmas party with carol-singing, etc.

• Sowing 3 (S3) is the Warm Pool where there is Gospel content, e.g. a Discovery Bible Study[4], the Story Formed Way,[5] or the Alpha Course[6]. Now we are raising the spiritual temperature.

• Reaping (R) is the Hot Pool. There is Gospel content like the previous phase, but we are also giving an opportunity to respond. It is really important to intentionally invite people to say yes to Jesus.

• Keeping (K) is the last phase in this diagram. In this pool we help people to connect with the larger community, but the whole discipleship process doesn't stop here, it is just beginning. This is when we begin to equip people so they know how to grow and feed themselves (see Chapter 23), and so they are able to sow and reap with the next generation of believers (see Chapter 24).

Four Outcomes of Sowing

When we read the Parable of the Sower we can see there are four outcomes of sowing the seed. Seed that falls on a path, in rocky places, among thorns, and in good soil where it will multiply 30, 60 or 100 fold. Since the seed is the same, then what makes the difference is the soil. So basically we're looking for good soil.

Questions:

What is good soil?

How do we know if someone is ready to receive the seeds of the Gospel?

GROWING

Jesus told another parable about a man who sowed: "The Kingdom of God is like a farmer who scatters seed on the ground. Night and day, while he's asleep or awake, the seed sprouts and grows, but he does not understand how it happens. The earth produces the crops on its own. First a leaf blade pushes through, then the heads of wheat are formed, and finally the grain ripens. And as soon as the grain is ready, the farmer comes and harvests it with a sickle, for the harvest time has come." (Mark 4:26-29 NLT)

---

4 http://worldmissionsevangelism.com/discovery-bible-studies/

5 http://www.gcmcollective.org/article/story-formed-way/

6 https://alpha.org/

If seed falls in good soil it starts to grow. The parable shows us that there are phases in the growth process. We don't want to over-spiritualize the text, but we like to use these phases to understand what can happen when the seed of the Gospel falls in good soil.

Leaf - a leaf receives light from the sun and air to photosynthesize. The Person of Peace begins to receive from the Word and Spirit. He is attracted to truth. Leaves turn towards the sun. He begins to receive the truth and understanding begins to grow.

Head - the kernel is where the energy of the sun and air begins to become part of the plant. The Person of Peace begins to own the truth as something he is beginning to believe for himself.

Grain - by the power of the sun, photosynthesis has changed the plant and it is now ripe wheat. The truth is fully part of the Person of Peace and they have become fruitful. The truth is no longer something he simply believes as true, but it defines him and his purpose (both as seed and wheat). He is ready to submit his life to the One who is Truth and bear good fruit that lasts.

REAPING - HARVEST TIME

It is at harvest time that the farmer makes a decision. He knows when it is time to reap the harvest. The harvester brings the sickle and the wheat is separated from the ground. The old life is cut off and the corn is reaped. Similar to a harvester, the discipler needs to be able to discern when the Person of Peace is ready to make a decision to follow Jesus; when he is ready for the Gospel to define his identity.

Not only is this person becoming a Christian with a new identity and new life. He carries the DNA to reproduce himself and in time he will be sowing seed into others and reaping changed lives.

A Reaping Tool

'Jesus at the Door' is a tool developed by Scott McNamara.[7] The whole approach is based on Revelation 3:20 that says: "Here I am! I stand at the door and knock. If anyone hears my voice and opens the door, I will come in and eat with that person, and he with me." It assumes God is already at work in people and the only thing we need to do is to find the people who are ready to open the door of their heart. In the Bible we can see this approach when Jesus met Zacchaeus, the tax collector (Luke 19), and the Samaritan woman at the well (John 4). They were both ready to acknowledge who Jesus is and to let him into their lives. We have seen great results from going out on the streets with a drawing of Jesus knocking on the door (see picture on this page) and asking specific questions.[8]

An Important Lesson

Sometimes we sow and water the seeds, but someone else will reap. Often we don't know it. However, when we do, it can be hard to see that we put a lot of effort but someone else will see the fruit. That can be hard, but it is okay. Why? Because the whole process has been governed by God. Paul writes: "What, after all, is Apollos? And what is Paul? Only servants, through whom you came to believe—as the Lord has assigned to each his task. I planted the seed, Apollos watered it, but God has been making it grow. So neither the one who plants nor the one who waters is anything, but only

---

7 http://jesusatthedoor.com

8 http://plantthefoxes.com/post/138797142977/tools-for-the-streets-jad

God, who makes things grow. The man who plants and the man who waters have one purpose, and each will be rewarded according to his own labor." (1 Corinthians 3:5-8)

HELPFUL DIAGRAMS

Although a diagram is a simplified picture of reality, it can help us to gain more insight in processes. We're aware that the reality is often more blurry and not as 'black and white' as a diagram. We find the three following diagrams helpful in our understanding of peoples' faith journey.

Five Thresholds People Need to Pass

People who become a Christian seem to pass through five distinct stages. The five thresholds of postmodern conversion (see picture)[9] are concepts developed by Don Everts and Doug Schaupp in their book, *I Once Was Lost.* [10] Understanding this process will help you to notice where someone is on his/her journey and how to encourage and challenge them.

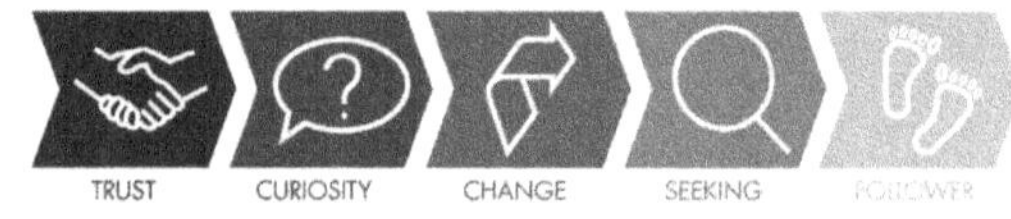

Threshold 1: Trusting a Christian - moving from distrust to trust

Threshold 2: Becoming Curious - moving from complacent (satisfaction with oneself) to curious

Threshold 3: Opening Up to Change - moving from being closed to being open to change in life

Threshold 4: Seeking After God - moving from meandering to seeking

Threshold 5: Following Jesus - crossing the threshold of the Kingdom itself and becoming a disciple

The Engel Scale

The Engel Scale (by James F. Engel) is a really helpful diagram to see how people move from having a vague awareness of a supreme being and no knowledge of the Gospel to becoming a committed follower of Jesus. Becoming aware of this scale helps us understand that sometimes we are only bringing a Person of Peace one step closer to knowing Jesus. Below is a picture of the Engel Scale, modified by Clive Calver and Nick Lear. We added two critical phases: baptism (12) and discipling others (17).

18. Discipling others
17. Ongoing growth
16. Share with others
15. Learn disciplines
14. Learn basics of faith
13. Experience life change
12. Baptism
11. Gain confidence in their decision
10. Decision to surrender to Jesus
9. Accept implications of becoming Christian
8. Acceptance of Christian truth
7. Understand implications of truth about Jesus
6. Grasp truth about Jesus
5. Investigating Jesus
4. Interest in Jesus
3. Contact with Christians
2. Some awareness of God
1. No awareness of God

THE DISCIPLESHIP PROCESS

Another diagram, from Caesar Kalinowski, describes the whole discipleship process, from making a first connection with someone, to equipping them to become a disciple-maker.[11]

The first step is to go from having a few connections to many connections. Then you move from natural

---

9 http://evangelism.intervarsity.org/resource/5-thresholds-postmodern-conversion-overview

10 D. Everts and D. Schaupp. *I Once Was Lost. What Postmodern Skeptics Taught Us About Their Path to Jesus.*

11 Shown at the Launch Learning Community, Sheffield Autumn 2016

conversations, where you talk about everyday life topics, to spiritual conversations. Somewhere in this process you'll find out if people are ready to become part of a community where you invite them on a spiritual journey. The ultimate goal is to disciple them so that they become disciple-makers themselves.

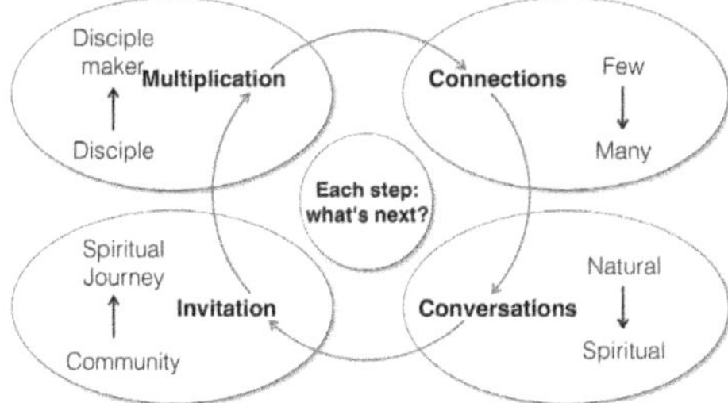

Conversations

If it is hard for you to talk to strangers this could be helpful:

- Be interested and take initiative!
- Notice what is unique about them.
- Notice if they need help and go help them.
- Talk about what you are experiencing now: e.g. standing in a line, taking a bus ride, today's weather, the smell of bread from a bakery, positive comments about their dog, admire their baby, etc.

How to introduce a spiritual dimension in your conversations: Our spiritual life needs to be authentic and visible. When we are full of Jesus then this is what will come out. But how do make our faith more visible?

1. Establish a Prayer Life

- Pray without ceasing. "Rejoice always; pray continually; give thanks in all circumstances, for this is God's will for you in Christ Jesus." (1 Thessalonians 5:16-18). Ask Jesus to help you do this and make that a regular prayer! Pray that when people meet you they would experience the presence of Jesus.
- Make thankfulness a discipline, when you wake up, leave the house, arrive somewhere, and go to bed.
- Get into the habit of asking God to bless people as you go through the day.
- Talk to him about what you are doing.
- Pray for each other and other Christians, make

opportunities, when leaving the house, when things come up.

- Spend quality time with Him, reading the Word, worshiping, listening to music, and sharing your heart with Him as you journal. This will get you praying and will make your relationship with Jesus more everyday.

2. Get Used to Talking About Your Spiritual Life

- When Jesus is central to your life it will be more natural to talk about Him to other people.
- Talk about your heart and what God is saying to non-Christians, even though it may seem strange. Just do it!
- Share and talk about Him and what He is saying as though He is someone solid and present and part of your ordinary life.
- Be quick to pray for each other.

All this prepares you for spiritual dialogue. When it feels normal for you to talk about spiritual things, it will feel much more normal to the person to whom you are talking.

3. Inviting Dialogue

These are five ways you can do this:
I. With a Passing Person - someone you might not see again
II. With a Permanent Person - someone who you will see again regularly
III. Sharing Our Peace - a personal current experience
IV. Sharing Our Good News - our personal overall experience
V. Sharing Our Hope - our personal future experience

I. With a Passing Person
Just go for it and ask them if you can share something. "I was just praying for you and I thought God might want to say..." or " I noticed you look as though you have a bad back, could I pray for you?"

II. With a Permanent Person
When an issue comes up (anxiety, politics, kids at school, etc) simply ask if they have faith; listen to what

they say; listen for the point of connection. Where does what they say reflect something of the Kingdom? For example justice, mercy, beauty, or love. Join in with this and share how it resonates with you.

III. Sharing Our Peace - a personal current experience
Examples are:
- Sharing about where I am trusting God at the moment. E.g. I'm trusting God to help me find a job. Sharing my gratitude.
- Vulnerability - show your trouble or grief in the presence of other people

IV. Sharing Our Good News - our personal overall experience
1 Peter 3:15 says: "But in your hearts set apart Christ as Lord. Always be prepared to give an answer to everyone who asks you to give the reason for the hope that you have. But do this with gentleness and respect."

What is Your Good News?
- What does walking with Jesus mean to you right now?
- What is good news to the person you're talking to?
- It is important to listen with our hearts. Ask God to show us what that person needs. There's no point giving people news that means nothing to them.

Sharing Our Good News in Different Ways:
- God is loving and just loves us as we are.
- God values us we are his joy.
We are all uniquely special to God.
- God has enough for us.
- He has a secure plan for us and includes everyone who wants to be 'in'.
- He wants to fill us with joy and peace and set us free from fear.
- God gives us life, life and more life. He is life power itself.
- He will bring harmony and unity to everything,
- He is peace.
- He will make all things (including us) perfect and just.

Concrete Examples:
- Neighbor: God is fun, loves community, it is ok to pray for a job.
- My friend: God can make all things right and there is a place for her = she belongs.
- Colleague: God loves her just as she is, no need to prove herself.
- Man at the airport - there is a place for him, God welcomes him.

Sharing Our Good News by Demonstration:
- Good News can be demonstrated by our presence.
- Ongoing prayer: people meet Jesus when they meet us.
- On the street: with our neighbors in particular, our lives are authentic and they can see that God is welcoming, loving, fun, generous, consistent and kind.
- Offer to pray whenever you can as this will give the person you are with an experience of the Holy Spirit and the presence of Jesus. It will also expose them to your relationship with Jesus.

Sharing our Good News - with People of Peace:
- Look for people who actually want to know what you think.
- Look for people who still come nearer when they see, hear and know what following Jesus means to you.
- Know the 'Big Story' - the meta narrative.
- Learn to tell the 'Big Story' like you would explain a movie, show people it is their story.

V. Sharing Our Hope - our personal future experience
- Our hope is about our future.
- It's our security that we are going to heaven.
- It's based on Jesus dying on the cross for us.
- It's available to anyone who chooses to depend on him, ask for his forgiveness, and choose make following him the center of their lives.

Questions

What part of the truth ripened in our lives are we sowing?

Where and when do we sow?

As we are wheat we can lay our lives down: be buried to be seed or/and be crushed to be flour to become bread - the word lived out. Where are we laying our lives down and seeing them become bread of truth to others?How able are we to read the signs of the harvest and know when the truth is owned and compels a person to follow Jesus?

CHAPTER 23

DISCIPLING NEW BELIEVERS

After people come to faith, the process continues. They need people around them who will raise them to become mature Christians who are able to feed themselves, feed others and reproduce themselves. We need to make disciples, who make disciples, who make disciples.

There are two things the enemy doesn't want to happen:
1. For someone become a Christian
2. For a new Christian to become more like Jesus, because that's a dangerous thing

Around both of these processes, becoming a Christian and becoming more like Jesus, we can expect opposition or spiritual warfare. That's why identity confirmation is so important.

THE NEED TO KNOW YOUR NEW IDENTITY

It is no coincidence that Jesus said, "Therefore go and make disciples of all nations, baptizing them in the name of the Father and the son and of the Holy Spirit" (Matthew 28:19). The first priority for new believers is to be immersed in the identity of the Father, Son and Spirit. This immersing is like dyeing clothes. The person is the cloth and they are to be completely united and covered in the name of the Father. They have the family name and identity.

"He is the Father from whom every family in heaven and on earths derives it's name" (Ephesians 3:15). His name is our identity, we are his royal sons and daughters,

full of his Spirit, we are immersed in Jesus' identity, the servant ruler King. We need to help our disciples immerse themselves in the Truth of who they have become.

The enemy uses temptation, deception and accusation to keep us from knowing our identity and walking in God's authority as a Christian. If we don't know how to deal with this, then 'strongholds' can been formed in our minds. A stronghold is a metaphor which the apostle Paul explains as follows: "We demolish arguments and every pretension that sets itself up against the knowledge of God, and we take captive every thought to make it obedient to Christ" (2 Corinthians 10:5). These 'arguments' are the philosophies, reasonings, and schemes of the world. The "pretensions" have to do with anything proud, human-centered, and self-reliant.

We need to tear down such strongholds by rejecting the lie or ungodly beliefs and applying the truth, which is found in the Word of God. In Romans 12:2 Paul writes: "Do not conform any longer to the pattern of this world, but be transformed by the renewing of your mind. Then you will be able to test and approve what God's will is— his good, pleasing and perfect will."

A helpful tool or process we use is the Freedom in Christ Discipleship Course (dvd's), which is based on Neil Anderson's teachings. Part of that is the '7 Steps to Freedom in Christ' which is a good way of helping people to renew their minds.[12]

EQUIP PEOPLE TO FEED THEMSELVES

We need to help people learn how to feed themselves. The spiritual life is similar to biological life. A baby needs milk because it can't have solid food and someone needs to give it to him. But when the baby grows it will be able to eat solid food and even to feed himself. Hopefully it won't stop here. When the child become older it will learn to do shopping, cooking for himself

---

12 www.freedominchrist.com. Helpful books by Neil Anderson are: *Victory Over the Darkness, Bondage Breaker and Discipleship Counseling.* The last one gives background information about the 7 steps.

and cooking for others. Beyond that we expect that people will become parents and feed their children.

In 1 Corinthians 3:2 Paul uses this picture for our spiritual life. He talks about believers whom he gives milk instead of solid food. Hebrew 5:12 says the believers should be teachers by now who teach others the basic principles of God's Word. But they are not there yet. What they need to do is to take responsibility for their own growth, their own learning and start feeding themselves.

Many Scriptures describe the need to grow and mature spiritually:

- Ephesians 4:14-15 - Be no longer children, but grow up in Christ.
- 2 Peter 3:18 - "But grow in the grace and knowledge of our Lord and Savior Jesus Christ."
- 2 Thessalonians 1:3 - "We ought always to thank God for you, brothers, and rightly so, because your faith is growing more and more, and the love of every one of you has for each another is increasing."

Questions:
Are you flourishing in all the areas we have identified in the growth list?
What areas need attention?
How do you make your life transparent to others?

EQUIP PEOPLE TO REPRODUCE

Young Christians need to learn that they also have a responsibility to give what they have received. From the first day they are a follower of Jesus, they are part of the mission of Jesus. Even before young Christians have learned to be a disciple, some are already attractive to others and can see a harvest in their environment. This is great. As they learn to feed themselves spiritually, and learn to feed others, they will become consistently attractive to those who have been saved: "For we are to God the aroma of Christ among those who are being saved" (2 Corinthians 2:15). They becoming the seed and the bread, leading visible lives that will attract others to guide them through these stages of learning.

When we add two new phases to the diagram from the previous Chapter and replace the Keeping stage, then it could look like this; the inverted triangle is connected with another triangle with Feeding yourself (F1) and Feeding others (F2).

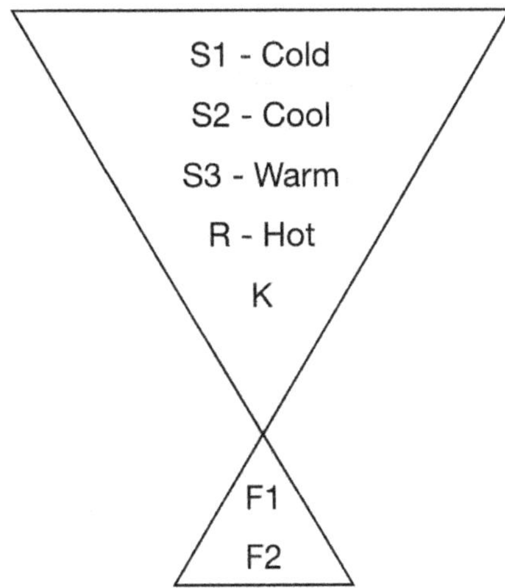

Questions:
Who is invited into your journey?
Do they know that this is an invitation, so that they can become mature in these areas and feed themselves and others?

HOW DO WE FEED OURSELVES?

What can we do to feed ourselves? And what is healthy for us? Again the biological world, which is often similar to our spiritual life, offers a helpful picture. Biologists tell us the main characteristics of living and growing organisms are Movement, Respiration, Sensitivity, Growth, Reproduction, Excretion and Nutrition. MRS GREN is an acronym often used to help remember all the features.[1]

We found the following explanation of these characteristics helpful.[2] At the left you'll find the biological processes we can see in living organisms and at the right the same processes but then related to our physical, spiritual, social and emotional life. If one of the processes is not working it will have an effect on the other parts. You can look at it as a whole, or pick one part and see how that is going in your (community) life.

Seven Processes of Life - Activities of Living Things

What Does Each Look Like in Life – Physical, Spiritual, Social, and Emotional?

Movement

All living things, people, animals and plants are moving. They are looking for food, running away from predators, searching for a mate, or trying to find better growing conditions. Plants and trees are moving as well. Some of them turn their stems, leaves or flower so that they point towards the sun and their roots move towards water.

Movement

Spiritually - Is it God you move towards? How do you move towards God?
Emotional - From where do we get our emotional support? Is it healthy?
Physical - Are we keeping our bodies healthy? How are we exercising? If we're not actually moving, our heart rate doesn't go up. Have we gone out for a walk, have we moved our body? Have we gone for a run? Have we lifted some weights?
Social - To which community do we belong? With whom are we connected? Do we have a healthy UP-IN-OUT balance?

---

1   Mike Breen and Steve Cockram, *Building a Discipling Culture*, p. 142-149.

2   http://www.whysotricky.com/about-us/making-things-simple/

Seven Processes of Life - Activities of Living Things

What Does Each Look like in Life – Physical, Spiritual, Social and Emotional?

Respiration

Being alive takes energy, so we draw energy from food in order to do things. Respiration is the process of extracting energy out of the food we eat.

What does each look like in life – physical, spiritual, social and emotional?

Respiration - Linked with Nutrition and Movement

Physically: It is linked with exercise and movement. We need oxygen to stay alive.

Spiritually: Are you breathing in the life of the Holy Spirit, the *pneuma*? The work of the Holy Spirit is always spoken of as breath: *ruach* in Hebrew, *pneuma* in Greek. So learn to breath in and out the Holy Spirit. Learn how to use the gifts of the Spirit and start training yourself.

Socially/emotionally: What are you breathing out? Encouragement, compassion, positive thoughts or envy, jealousy, anger, bitterness and relational dysfunction which may offend other people?

Sensitivity

One of the requirements of being alive is to be sensitive to our surroundings. To be aware of what's around us ensures we can keep out of danger and find food and shelter. Plants can sense where light is coming from and can therefore grow towards it to make the most of its energy.

Sensitivity

Sensitivity causes a movement or reaction. What do you respond to? To what things do you react positively and to what do you react negatively? What things make you respond, move towards them or move away?

Spiritually: Do we have sensitive hearts or hardened hearts? Are we sensitive for the still, small voice of God? Are we communicating with God - praying, listening and hearing. Are we thinking about prophecy - how to receive and process prophetic words given to us?

Physically: Are there unhealthy habbits?

Socially: You may want to move away from certain people, but maybe the Lord wants you to move towards them.

Emotionally: How do you think people react to you? Do people think you're an emotional drain, do they want to be with you, are you sensitive to their needs, do you pick up what they need?

Seven Processes of Life - Activities of Living Things

What Does Each Look Like in Life – Physical, Spiritual, Social and Emotional?

Growth

All living things grow, from tiny acorns to mighty oak trees, and from tiny babies into adults.

Growth

Spiritually: Look at your growth in the UP-IN-OUT, are you stretching yourself?

Socially: Are you growing in relationships, are you making new friends, are there friends you perhaps need to let go of in order to live a healthier lifestyle? Sometimes our orbits with people need to change. Are we helping each other grow?

Emotionally: Are you learning from your mistakes? Are you celebrating the success of others? Have you stopped complaining?

Reproduction

Living things can make more living things of the same type. Plants produce seeds, animals have babies, and microbes cut out the middle man (or woman) and divide into two.

Reproduction

Spiritually/Socially: Are you producing offspring? Are you living a life which other people want to imitate (not only Christians)? Are you boring? Don't live in a Christian ghetto! Go to the movies, visit art galeries, listen to good music, live a life that people will find interesting and attractive, a life they want to reproduce in their lives.

Emotionally: Are you reproducing a good emotional lifestyle?

Physically: Do people see you are living a healthy lifestyle? Reproduce every bit of your life and live an interesting life.

Seven Processes of Life - Activities of Living Things

What Does Each Look Like in Life – Physical, Spiritual, Social and Emotional?

Excretion – Removal of Waste Products
When living things respire (breathing) they create waste. This waste needs to be excreted, whether it is carbon dioxide from breathing or excess heat being lost continuously through our skin

Excretion
Physically - are you eating healthy food regularly, drinking plenty of water, and are you getting enough exercise so that your body is able to get rid of the waste/toxic products? Toxic products are poison and will have a detrimental effect.

Are you in control of the things you use which easily can become addictive: food, drinks, social media, games, chocolate, etc.?

Emotionally - Are you dealing with emotional baggage and hurts from the past which prevent you moving forward in a healthy way? Do you have people you trust who can help you deal with emotional issues?

Socially - Do you have a good social life? A balance of healthy relationships and people who affect your life in a positive way and encourage you. Perhaps there are relational difficulties or areas which need to be 'cleared out' or reconciled, etc?

Spiritually - Is all the spiritual stuff within you healthy? Or are you influenced by negativity, deception, or unholy thoughts? What do you need to clear out (excrete)? Maybe there are people you need to forgive, areas of sin for which you need to ask forgiveness? What about your attitude? Do you hold stuff against people based on bitterness or anger? What is the poisoning stuff in your body?

You have to deal with the toxins of your spiritual life. E.g. repentance of wrong thoughts, ungodly beliefs, sinful behavior, and forgiveness for self and others. Sometimes it is necessary to have indepth prayer or deliverance prayer to clear these things out.

Seven Processes of Life - Activities of Living Things

What Does Each Look Like in Life – Physical, Spiritual, Social and Emotional?

Nutrition - Taking in Nutrients/Food

In order to release energy from food, we need to continually take in that food. Animals must consume other living things as food. Plants generate their own food through photosynthesis, combining simple chemicals and energy from sunlight to make nutrients.

Nutrition

Jesus said in Luke 4:4: "It is written: 'Man does not live on bread alone.'" Physical nourishment isn't sufficient for a healthy life. Man has also spiritual needs. We need to be fed by Jesus every day! "I am the bread of life." (John 6:48). Feed yourself with God's truth by reading God's Word, renew your thinking with His truth and start acting upon it, like Jesus did.

Spiritually: what is good spiritual nutrition? People in our culture have the tendency to pick and chose from a variety of sources, whatever catches their attention. The question is, are you getting a well-balanced diet?

Socially: Do we eat with others? Do we read together, the Bible or other books?

Emotionally: How are we feeling when we talk about food? What do we do when we are emotional? Is God our only source for support? Are we feeding ourselves with God and are we feeding together?

Physically: Are we feeding the poor? Are we feeding people both physically and spiritually, including people who don't know Jesus?

CHAPTER 24

MULTIPLYING DISCIPLES

The main challenge for discipleship is that we (as the first-generation disciples) learn how to disciple the second-generation, that generation learns to disciple the third, and so on. This won't happen automatically, so we need to be intentional. We need to know what we're looking for, in other words, what is the outcome we want to see?

AREAS OF DISCIPLESHIP

After someone has made the choice to be a follower of Jesus we would like to see them grow in the following Covenant and Kingdom traits:

Covenant Traits
- Know who he/she is in Christ (identity)
- Inner healing, deliverance prayer if necessary
- Renewing of the mind
- Character: e.g. thankfulness, patience, trust, provision, forgiveness, generosity, serving, kindness, contentment, humility, perseverance and freedom
- Know how to feed themselves: hearing God, reading the Bible, worship and prayer (personal and corporate) - UP
- Taking responsibility for their own (spiritual) lives
- Rhythms of work and rest
- Being part of a community (IN) - live out the values of that community (core values, rhythms)
- Know his/her fivefold and calling

Kingdom Traits
- Living out the values of blessing others, hospitality, forgiveness, reconciliation, etc.
- Inviting and challengiung others
- Showing God's love to others - OUT
- Know how to share peace, Good News and hope
- Know how to feed others (word, prayers, worship, prophecy and sharing the Gospel)
- Inviting others to follow and start living a missional lifestyle together

An extra area of attention may be the phase of life in which a person finds himself. In each phase you have certain aspects in which you can disciple people: student life, early adulthood, relationships, marriage, being single, moving to another country, starting a missional community or household, etc.

When can we speak of multiplication? It is not just when one of our disciples starts their own community, multiplication is also happening when your disciples begin imitating you. This is similar to a family with children where the older siblings help to raise the younger ones.

These are important principles if you want to see multiplication:[13]
- I can't give what I don't have.
- I multiply who I am, not just what I do.
- I can only invest in a few.
- I can't ask people to go where I haven't been myself.

Looking at these basic principles we need to realize we can't approach discipleship as a one-size-fits-all program where people attend ten sessions and then they 'are discipled'. It is always a tailor-made process. Although there power in being part of a community, we can't close our eyes to the individual processes, simply because we are all different and have different backgrounds and brokenness in our lives. Therefore the main questions we need to ask are:
- Where are people in their faith journey?
- Where are they in their understanding of missional discipleship?
- Where do they need to grow?

---

13   Chad Norris at Prophetic Conference, "Building Deep Friendship with God," Sheffield, Leaders night 16/03/17

DIFFERENT PHASES IN THE PROCESS

In building a discipling culture, the process of discipleship is divided in four phases for the disciple (D1 - D4) and four phases for the leader (L1 -L4). This is combined in one diagram, the Square.[14] Below we show both of the viewpoints in two separate diagrams: 'the four stages of competence' and 'the gradual release of responsibility.'

The Four Stages of Competence[15]

A healthy disciple goes through the following four phases:

- Unconscious incompetence (D1) - the individual does not understand or know how to do something and does not necessarily recognize the deficit. They may deny the usefulness of the skill. The individual must recognize their own incompetence, and the value of the new skill, before moving on to the next stage. The length of time an individual spends in this stage depends on the strength of the desire to learn.
- Conscious Incompetence (D2) - though the individual does not understand or know how to do something, he or she does recognize the deficit, as well as the value of a new skill in addressing the deficit. The making of mistakes can be integral to the learning process at this stage.
- Conscious Competence (D3) - the individual understands or knows how to do something. However, demonstrating the skill or knowledge requires concentration. It may be broken down into steps, and there is heavy conscious involvement in executing the new skill.
- Unconscious Competence (D4) - the individual has had so much practice with a skill that it has become "second nature" and can be performed easily. As a result, the skill can be performed while executing another task.

Gradual Release of Responsibility[16]

The 'Gradual Release of Responsibility (GRR)' model is a specific teaching style in which four successive phases are distinguished. The aim is that the teacher supports the pupil until he is able to do the task independent of the teacher.

The picture[17] on this page shows the four phases which are named at the bottom, 'I' is the teacher/discipler and 'you' the pupil/disciple.

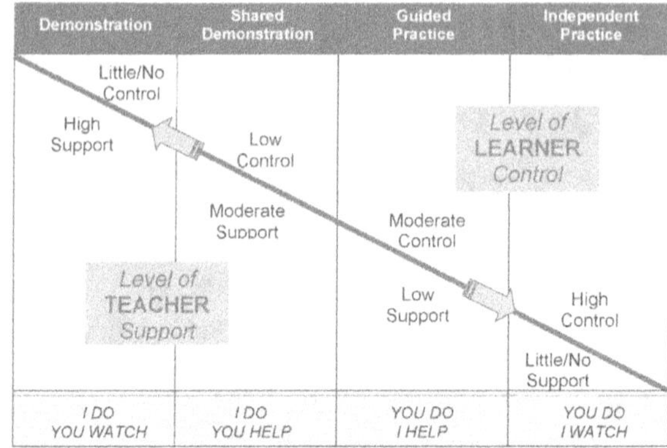

In the diagram, the level of support the teacher is giving goes from high support (upper left corner) to little or no support (lower right corner), while the level of control for the pupil goes from no control (upper left corner) to high control (lower right corner).

When we look at the 'square' from a leader/discipler perspective (L) then the four sides represents the four stages of gradual release of responsibility that both the leader/discipler and disciple needs to go through.

- L1 - I do, you watch
- L2 - I do, you help
- L3 - You do, I help
- L4 - You do, I watch

If you are familiar with 'The Square' then you know that

---

14   Mike Breen and Steve Cockram, *Building a Discipling Culture*, p 99-112

15   https://en.wikipedia.org/wiki/Four_stages_of_competence

16   https://en.wikipedia.org/wiki/Gradual_release_of_responsibility

17   Source: http://www.literacyleader.com/node/477

the D and L phases are supposed to happen at the same time. However my experience is that people can enter D2 (conscious incompetence) in any of the learning phases where the discipler is leading the disciple. The most obvious one is probably when the leader operates in L3 and where the disciple gets more responsibility. These are the phases through which a disciple needs to

When leading people you need to know in which stage of competence the disciple is and it is necessary to adjust your leadership style accordingly.

These are the phases and leadership styles through which a discipler needs to progress:[18]

Disciple Phase
D1: Confident and incompetent
D2: Not enthusiastic and incompetent
D3: Growing confidence
D4: The end is in sight

Discipler Phase and Leadership Style
L1: Directive
L2: Visionary/coach
L3: Pastoral/consensus
L4: Delegation

CONDITIONS FOR A HEALTHY PROCESS

To make discipleship a success there are a few conditions we need to be aware of. To start with the discipler:
- Needs to live a visible life, otherwise the disciple can't see anything (I do, you watch).
- Needs to live an invitational life, the disciple needs an opportunity to join me (I do, you help).
- Needs to live a faith-filled life, trusting God: we can do these things together (You do I help).
- Needs to live a generous life: I will watch you and I will celebrate your life as it flourishes independently of me and is seen by others (You do I watch).
- Needs to release completely, give up control, maintain commitment to my disciples.

For the disciple there are also some areas to be aware of: The disciple will need to die to perfectionism, control, personal success and image.

There are a few phases which can be difficult:
- D2 - Conscious Incompetence: in this phase you realize that it's harder then you thought.
- D3 - Conscious Competence: in this phase you start doing things differently, but it will take effort.
- L1 - I do, you watch: you need be become a learner again. You have to give up control. This is especially hard when you've been a leader in L4 yourself.

Questions
*What is your vision for discipleship? Who are the people you are discipling/want to disciple?
How intentionally are you in discipling them?
Where are they in their process, in which phase(s)?
What do you (personally) need to disciple them well?*

---

18   Mike Breen and Steve Cockram, *Building a Discipling Culture*, p 99-112

STEPPING STONE SEVEN

STARTING STEP BY STEP

CHAPTER 25

FROM VISION TO REALITY

In recent years we have started two missional initiatives. The first one was in Sheffield and we did it together with Sharon, co-author of this book. The second initiative is our current community in Gouda. This time we were on our own as Sharon has continued to live in Sheffield.

I (Mark) remembered from the first time that, even though the three of us were the initiators, it was really a learning season for me and Jacolien in which we went from D1-unconsciously incompetent to D3-consciously competent (see Chapter 24, Multiplying Disciples). We had the privilege of being discipled by someone with years of community experience. I must say that it has been very educational and an indispensable experience. While I used to work directly from theory, I have now learned from others in practice.

Another major advantage of practical learning is that we are now better able to contextualize what we have learned to the situation in the Netherlands. Apparently England and the Netherlands are very similar, but there are quite a few cultural differences.

In this seventh Stepping Stone we briefly indicate which practical steps you can take to begin living a missionary lifestyle. If you're anything like me, this is probably the chapter you are tempted to start with. You want to get started as soon as possible and you don't feel like going through a lot of theory first. How hard can it be, right?

This chapter contains references to earlier chapters in the book so you can read more about the subject in question. I would advise you to actually do this. The information there is very useful, so take advantage of it. I wish I had had that information sooner, then I probably would have made fewer mistakes. Be sure to read Chapter 1, Missional Discipleship, since it is the foundation of what we do.

In that chapter you can read that God invites us to be part of His mission: to proclaim the Kingdom of God and make disciples. This is not optional, but a command that Jesus himself gave in Matthew 28.

Of course you can shape this in several ways. We chose to integrate this assignment into our daily life in such a way that it is also doable for others. We cannot expect others to do something that we do not do ourselves. I can't tell from a platform what church members should do, without doing it myself.

In concrete terms, this means for us that we have a normal (albeit part-time) job. We do not have an exceptional 'ministry,' but try to give shape to Jesus' mission in everyday life. We also choose to do this together with others in what we call a missional community. Over the years we have discovered that a community is a good way to support the mission. Regardless of what name you give it, it is a group of people who share life with each other and live out God's mission together.

As a result, for us a missional community is not an end in itself, but the organizational structure we use to form a missionary family and to live a missionary life together with others (see Chapter 1). This chapter discusses a number of topics that are important when starting an initiative. This list is not intended to cover everything, but it does give a good start. The following topics will be discussed successively:

- Hearing God
- Vision
- Taking initiative
- Forming a Core Group
- UP-IN-OUT rhythms
- Values
- APEST and Myers Briggs
- Discipleship process
- General remarks

HEARING GOD

One of the most important things to start with is to learn to listen to God. We believe He still speaks today. You can do this as an individual, but also as a group. That way you can receive a vision and you can start working on it. It's nice to have a good idea, but a God idea is even better. You can read more in Chapter 8, Listening to God and Prophecy.

VISION

Like everything else, living a missional lifestyle with others starts with a vision (see also Chapter 15, Vision). Such is our vision: to make disciples who make disciples. The way we do that is by living a missional lifestyle, together with others in a missional community. By using the adjective missional we want to emphasize that we are part of God's mission.

TAKING INITIATIVE

It cannot stop with vision alone. There comes a time when you start to turn the vision into action. You will have to take initiative. This is easier for some than others. Especially for people who score high on the A and P in the APEST (see Chapter 18, The Fivefold roles of Ephesians 4), it will take little effort to start something new. The challenge for them, however, is to ensure that more people participate and that the initiative is not a short-lived hype.

FORMING A CORE GROUP

Part of taking the initiative is to invite others, starting with those who will join you as part of the core of the missional family, which we call the core group for convenience. Most likely these will be Christians. In Chapter 21, Calling People, you will find helpful criteria for this. We prefer to speak of a core group than of a core team or even a leadership team. Even though there are many similarities with a team, such as cooperation and achieving goals, the big difference is sharing life together. Basically it is the difference between what we call Covenant Relationships and Kingdom Activities. We

will come back to this later in this chapter.

An example that might help clarify things is Jesus and his disciples. We don't see them as a team with team meetings, do we? jesus described them as a family. Language creates culture, so it's important to choose the right words and names.

When you have invited people to participate, it is wise to use a trial period. During that time people can experience what it is like to form a community. People are probably excited, but don't really know what they're getting into, they're unconsciously incompetent. It is the first phase (D1) of the Discipleship Square (Chapter 24, Multiplying Disciples). We use a period of about six months. After those six months you can have an evaluation and choice moment

After the core group has been formed, you can start inviting others. We consciously distinguish between participants who are part of the core group and other participants.

A few important tips:

Married Couples
If it involves couples then invite both partners, because it is a lifestyle and that will also have an effect on a partner.

Discipleship Square
Make sure you explain the participants the four D phases of discipleship (again Chapter 24). It is important that people understand that they do not know exactly where they are stepping in and that after the D1 phase inevitably follows D2, Conscious Incompetence. This is often not a pleasant phase, but unfortunately unavoidable.

D2 Phase
It is important to know that not everyone is willing to go through the D2 phase. Of course you hope they will, but that is not always the case. This is not a bad thing. People have the choice to go through the D2 phase or

to drop out. Give people that freedom and realize it's not up to you.

However, the result is that you have to say goodbye to this person. If you do not do the latter, you run the risk that you will compromise to 'keep' participants in the community. That will keep them in D1 and they will unconsciously remain incompetent. Subsequently, there is a good chance that they will (consciously or unconsciously) introduce what they are skilled at in the community. The risk is that the community will not function as it was intended.

Do Not Start in D3/L3

Because people often want to participate in the decision-making process, we see many initiatives starting in phase D3/L3 (see again Chapter 24). The leadership style is that of consensus. In the start-up phase of a community, this is not a good idea. Not everyone can foresee the consequences of a decision.

An example: we believe it is important to start with the OUT as soon as possible, but the majority of the group may not feel like doing this. So if you let it depend on the group, you will probably not be doing any OUT until people think they are ready. Our experience is that it is difficult to get the OUT rhythms in place when you are a few months doing UP and IN rhythms. It is therefore not wise to let people who are in the D1 phase participate in the decision-making process.

Character for Competence

It is important to consider a person's character when determining whether someone is suitable to participate. I believe that good character is more important than competence (see Chapter 21 again). My sense is that learning competencies is easier than changing one or more character traits. So someone has to accept that he or she starts in D1. From experience I know that this can be difficult. Understanding this journey from Unconscious Incompetence to Unconscious Competence is essential. Chapter 24 is really a must read!

UP-IN-OUT RHYTHMS

In order to invite people properly, it is important that you have some idea what you are invting them into. Most helpful in this are UP-IN-OUT rhythms (see Chapter 6, Balanced and Integrated Relationships and also Chapter 7 UP, Chapter 9 IN and Chapter 10 OUT). In short, UP is about our (individual and collective) relationship with God, IN is about our relationships with each other in the community, and OUT is about relationships with people who don't know Jesus yet.

A few important principles regarding UP-IN-OUT:

Covenant Relationships and Kingdom Activities

We need to distinguish between the relational aspects of faith, both with God and with each other, on the one hand, and activities on the other. Everything needs to start with our relationship with God. Activities and pursuits can arise from this. This is a really important point because you can quickly get bogged down in a collection of activities, which are good in themselves, but sometimes are just that, activities.

Regularity and Balance

It's not about the quantity, but the regularity and balance between the three UP-IN-OUT parts. Make sure that all three are present at least once a month, for example.

Structured and Spontaneous

With everyone's busy schedules you have to plan most things, but it's also important to stay spontaneous. This can be done very easily by inviting others to something that you already planned to do. Please note that not everyone has to participate or be present for every activity.

Purpose and Play

Make sure you don't just see each other around a task or some 'official' meeting. Make time to relax together. Do fun things and get to know each other in a different way.

People of Peace

The principle of people of peace is valuable both for starting a community and later for the OUT. At the beginning you are looking for a few people (Christians) who are open to you and want to participate. Later, as you move OUT, you are looking for people (who are not yet Christians) who are open to get to know Jesus. The contact with a person of peace will probably come through one of the community members. Make sure that this person also comes into contact with other community members.

Permanent and Passing

With the OUT it is helpful to take into account the distinction between permanent and passing relationships. Permanent ones are, for example, family, neighbors and colleagues. You see these people more often and you have a long-term relationship with them. Passing relationships are people you may only see once or a few times.

When There Is No Specific OUT (Yet)

When you as a group are part of a larger community, it is natural to choose a specific target group, such as a Neighborhood or a Network. When you're not part of a bigger picture, it's better to let that go and basically focus on people who cross your path. This can be local residents or people from the networks you are part of and of course people with a certain need. What works best is just to see if someone is a person of peace.

Be Wise About What You Invite (Non-Believing) People To

If you have not yet had a spiritually substantive conversation with someone then it is probably better to invite this person to something without explicit Gospel content. Let someone acclimate to the community, as it were. Of course, be clear from the start that you are a Christian community, so that there is no unwanted 'bait-and-switch' effect.

We use a simple scheme that you can find in Chapter 22, Sowing, Growing, and Reaping. This describes who you should invite for what. In this chapter we also mention Discovery Bible Study. Since we have had positive experiences with DBS, we decided to devote Chapter 26 to explaining how it works.

VALUES

When you have been gathering as a community for between six and twelve months, it is good to define the values (See also Chapter 20, Personal and Shared Values). Everyone lives from a set of values. It is good to recognize this in each other, but also to determine which values we consider important as a community and, above all, how we want to give them practical shape. It is also nice to know who already has such a common value by nature. That helps to enjoy it together. Suppose you value hospitality as a community, then someone who is naturally hospitable can help others to shape this together.

APEST AND MYERS BRIGGS

Living alongside one another in community becomes easier when you know each others' gifting and personalities in both the APEST and Myers Briggs. In brief: APEST (see Chapter 18, The Fivefold gifts of Ephesians 4) is the English abbreviation for the five ministries in Ephesians 4, Apostle, Prophet, Evangelist, Shepherd (Pastor), and Teacher. All five are necessary for building up the church and they all have their qualities and pitfalls.

In addition, Myers Briggs Type Indicator (MBTI) is very helpful. It is an instrument that is used worldwide for personal development, team development and organizational development. MBTI is based on a person's preferences on four aspects:
1. Where does someone get his/her energy from and how does he/she recharge?
2. How does someone collect information?
3. How does someone make decisions?
4. How does someone prefer to order his/her live, in a planned or flexible way?

If you want to know more about this, please contact Jacolien at www.originalcoaching.nl or Sharon at www.sharonearlconsulting.com.

DISCIPLESHIP PROCESS

When the goal of the community is to make disciples who make disciples then it is wise to have a discipleship process. What we have learned over the years is that such a process is tailor-made and certainly not a 'one-size-fits-all,' since every person is different, is in a different phase, develops in a different way, and/or learn new things differently. Despite that, you can roughly distinguish a few target groups:

- Christians - they can be discipled in specific topics in which they want to grow, discipling others and community life
- Newcomers/young believers - they should be discipled in the basic knowledge and skills of the Christian faith, such as reading the Bible, praying and listening to God's voice.
- Children - the same applies to them as to newcomers/young believers
- Teenagers - they too can be discipled in specific topics in which they want to grow, discipling others and community life

You will have to think about what the discipleship process might look like for these groups. An important tip regarding this process: even though different people are in different phases, don't let the 'slowest' or the least experienced or knowledgeable guide you in what you want to do. Make sure that there is room for someone to set their own pace and whether or not they 'participate' in certain parts.

Principle of Invitation and Challenge

Two important principles are those of Invitation and Challenge (see also Chapter 5, Invitation to Relationship and Challenge to Change). These two principles can be found in Mark 1:16-18, where we see Jesus saying to the brothers Simon and Andrew: 'Come, follow me! I will make you fishers of men." In this passage we often see only the challenge Jesus gave: I will make you fishers of men. But Jesus began with an invitation to come to him and follow him. As Jesus invites Simon and Andrew, he invites us too. He cares about the relationship. When discipling other people, it is important that we start by inviting people into our lives, spending time together, getting to know one another, encouraging one another, and loving one another.

To grow as a disciple, we also need challenges. Just receiving invitations creates a cozy and comfortable atmosphere that can be fun for a while, but it doesn't help us change. Challenge is about change. Or as C. S. Lewis said, "Every Christian must become a little Christ." The purpose of change is clear: we want to grow in character to be more like Jesus. This internal change also affects how we will do things.

GENERAL REMARKS

Community Participation Is Voluntary At All Times.
Working with mandatory attendance does not work. Do not communicate this indirectly either. You do need a core group that is committed to each other. When participants decide to stop for whatever reason after a while, bless them and say goodbye in a positive way.

Not Everyone Has to Be Present Everytime
The core group, 'spiritual parents,' set the rhythm and the rest are invited to participate. Continuity is more important than quantity (number of participants participating).

Proximity Facilitates Community Life.
When you live close to each other it is easier to live together missionally and to meet each other spontaneously than when you live further away.

Holidays Are a Great Way to Do OUT.
Holidays are a time when people naturally gather so it a great way to build community with people of peace. The lesson we have learned is to be sensitive to people's schedules and be willing to adjust accordingly. For example: is it nice to organize something around

Christmas, but most people are away on Christmas Day and New Year's Eve, so organize something the weekend before.

Low Costs and Little Organization.
Because the focus is not on building a strong 'center' with paid employees who have to keep all kinds of programs running, or on the purchase of a building, the costs can remain low and you don't have to spend a lot of time on organization.

Your People Are My People.
The power of community is a place where people of peace are invited to meet the other people in the group. Probably the greatest chemistry will exist between the member of the community and her or his person of peace, but it is important that the whole community welcoming to everyone, include those who are people of peace to others.

CHAPTER 26

DISCOVERY BIBLE STUDY

In Chapter 22 we explain when to do activities with or without Gospel content. One of the most effective activities with Gospel content that we have experienced is Discovery Bible Study (DBS). DBS is extremely helpful for inviting non-believers for the following reasons:

- Participants learn to read the Bible for themselves
- They get the space to share what appeals to them
- They are encouraged to do something concrete in response
- Because no 'expert knowledge' may be brought in from outside the Bible story, there is no 'power relationship' (or inequality) based on biblical knowledge. This creates a culture of mutual discovery.

Here's how it works:

- Ask a participant to read aloud the chosen Bible passage
- Ask another participant to read aloud the same passage again, preferably from a different translation. The Message is an excellent choice!
- Everyone closes their Bible
- Explain that we will now try to tell the story together in our own words
- Ask a participant to start and when he/she is ready you can ask if others have anything to add.

After the reading and retelling of the story you discuss the following 5 questions:

Minor rule: we are concentrating on this story, which means that you are not allowed to add any other passages or knowledge from the Bible to this story.

1. What does this say about people? (specifically in this story and/or in general)

2. What does this say about God, Jesus or the Holy Spirit? (depending on who's in it)

3. What does it have to say to you? (give participants a moment to think about this)

4. What are you going to do in response? (It is good to be as concrete as possible. It is also good to follow up with people for accountability with the simple question, "How did it go?")

5. Who else should hear this? / Who are you going to tell this to?

Sometimes we like to add a sixth question:

6. Is there anything what stood out for us as a community?

Note: you will probably have to call on people to answer the first few questions. Later it may become more natural. Incidentally, not everyone has to formulate an answer to the first two questions. Of course you want everyone to answer the last two questions.

Closing: End with prayer – this can of course be done in various ways.

TIPS

1. Ask questions, don't teach (let the Scripture teach, not you)

2. Focus on obedience, not just knowledge (knowledge comes best from obedience, not the opposite)

3. Pass on leadership (don't let it depend on you)

4. Stick to the story (that keeps everyone engaged)

5. Keep it simple so it's easy to reproduce (don't complicate the process)

See Appendix 3 for Scripture passages you can use in Discovery Bible Study.

APPENDIX 1

Recommended Books

Building a Discipleship Culture, by Mike Breen and Steve Cockram
Covenant and Kingdom, by Mike Breen
The Forgotten Ways, Reactivating the Missional Church, by Alan Hirsch
Evangelism Strategies, by Bob and Mary Hopkins
My Sheep Have Ears, by Cath Livesey
On the Verge; a Journey into the Apostolic Future of the Church, by Alan Hirsch & Dave Ferguson
Primal Fire: Reigniting the Church With the Five Gifts of Jesus, by Neil Cole
Empowering Missional Disciples, by Bob Rognlien
Small is Big, Slow is Fast: Living and Leading Your Family and Community, by Caesar Kalinowski
The Permanent Revolution, by Alan Hirsch & Tim Catchim
The Tangible Kingdom; Creating Incarnational Community, by Hugh Halter and Matt Smay.
Culture of Honor: Sustaining a Supernatural Environment, by Danny Silk
Fathering Leaders, Motivating Mission, by David Devenish
The Cry for Spiritual Mothers and Fathers, by Larry Kreider
5Q, Reactivating the Original Intelligence and Capacity of the Body of Christ, by Alan Hirsch

APPENDIX 2

List of Values (in alphabetical order)

Abundance	Brilliance	Courtesy	Enthusiasm
Acceptance	Calmness	Craftiness	Environmentalism
Accessibility	Camaraderie	Creativity	Ethics
Accomplishment	Candor	Credibility	Excellence
Accountability	Care	Cunning	Excitement
Accuracy	Carefulness	Curiosity	Expectancy
Achievement	Certainty	Daring	Expediency
Acknowledgement	Challenge	Decisiveness	Experience
Activeness	Change	Decorum	Expertise
Adaptability	Charity	Deference	Exploration
Adoration	Charm	Delight	Expressiveness
Advancement	Cheerfulness	Dependability	Extroversion
Adventure	Clarity	Depth	Exuberance
Affection	Clear-mindedness	Desire	Fairness
Alertness	Cleverness	Determination	Faith
Altruism	Closeness	Devotion	Family
Amazement	Comfort	Dignity	Fascination
Ambition	Commitment	Diligence	Fearlessness
Amusement	Community	Direction	Fidelity
Anticipation	Compassion	Directness	Fierceness
Appreciation	Competence	Discipline	Firmness
Approachability	Concentration	Discovery	Fitness
Approval	Confidence	Diversity	Flexibility
Art	Conformity	Dreaming	Flow
Artistry	Congruency	Duty	Fluency
Assertiveness	Connection	Eagerness	Focus
Assurance	Consciousness	Ease	Fortitude
Attentiveness	Conservation	Ecstasy	Frankness
Attractiveness	Consistency	Education	Freedom
Availability	Contentment	Effectiveness	Friendliness
Awareness	Continuity	Efficiency	Friendship
Awe	Contribution	Elegance	Fun
Balance	Conviction	Empathy	Generosity
Beauty	Coolness	Encouragement	Giving
Belonging	Cooperation	Endurance	Grace
Benevolence	Correctness	Energy	Gratitude
Boldness	Country	Enjoyment	Growth
Bravery	Courage	Entertainment	Guidance

List of Values (continued)

Happiness	Liveliness	Potency	Security
Harmony	Logic	Power	Self-control
Health	Love	Practicality	Selflessness
Heart	Loyalty	Pragmatism	Self-respect
Helpfulness	Making a difference	Precision	Sensitivity
Heroism	Marriage	Preparedness	Serenity
Holiness	Mastery	Presence	Service
Honesty	Maturity	Pride	Sharing
Honor	Meaning	Privacy	Significance
Hopefulness	Meekness	Proactivity	Silence Simplicity
Hospitality	Modesty	Professionalism	Sincerity
Humility	Motivation	Prosperity	Skillfulness
Humor	Mysteriousness	Prudence	Solidarity
Imagination	Nature	Punctuality	Solitude
Impact	Neatness	Purity	Sophistication
Independence	Noncomformity	Rationality	Soundness
Individuality	Obedience	Realism	Spirit
Influence	Open-mindedness	Reasonableness	Spirituality
Ingenuity	Openness	Recognition	Spontaneity
Inquisitiveness	Optimism	Recreation	Stability
Insightfulness	Order	Reflection	Stillness
Inspiration	organization	Relaxation	Strength
Integrity	Originality	Reliability	Structure
Intellect	Outdoors	Relief	Success
Intensity	Partnership	Reputation	Support
Intimacy	Patience	Resilience	Surprise
Introversion	Passion	Resolution	Sympathy
Intuitiveness	Peace	Resolve	Synergy
Inventiveness	Perceptiveness	Resourcefulness	Teaching
Investing	Perfection	Respect	Teamwork
Involvement	Perseverance	Responsibility	Thankfulness
Joy	Persistence	Rest	Thoroughness
Justice	Persuasiveness	Reverence	Thoughtfulness
Keenness	Piety	Richness	Tidiness
Kindness	Playfulness	Sacrifice	Timeliness
Knowledge	Pleasantness	Sagacity	Traditionalism
Leadership	Pleasure	Satisfaction	Trust
Learning	Popularity	Science	Trustworthiness

List of Values (continued)

Truth
Understanding
Uniqueness
Unity
Usefulness
Utility
Variety
Victory
Virtue
Vision
Vitality
Volunteering
Warmheartedness
Warmth
Willingness
Wisdom
Wonder
Worthiness
Zeal

Scripture Passages for DBS

Hearing Gods Voice (8)
1 Samuel 3 – Samuel
Judges 6:11-40 – Gideon
Exodus 3-1-21 – Mozes
2 Samuel 7:1-17 – David
Acts 9:1-19 – Paul & Ananias
Acts 10:1-23, 3/7 – Peter and Cornelius (I)
Acts 10: 24-48 – Peter and Cornelius (II)
Acts 13:1-12 – Paul and Barnabas
Acts 16:1-15 – Paul's vision

Missional Stories (9)
John 3:1-21 – Jesus and Nicodemus
John 4:1-42 – Jesus and the woman
Acts 2:43-47 – The fellowship of believers
Acts 8:26-40 – Philip and the Ethiopian
Acts 10:1-23, 3/7 – Peter and Cornelius (I)
Acts 10: 24-48 – Peter and Cornelius (II)
Acts 16:11-15 – Paul and Lydia
Acts 16:16-34 – Paul, Silas and the Jailer
Acts18:1-28 – Aquila and Priscilla

The Following 90 Stories You Can Find on www.studies.discoverapp.org/series/
Creation to Christ (30)
Becoming disciples (9)
Training Laborers (10)
Stories of Hope (8)
Signs of John (8)
For Such a Time (9)
Commands of Christ (9)
Discover Christmas (7)

Scripture Passages for DBS (continued)

The Following 156 Stories You Can Find on www.kcunderground.org/dbs-process
10 Stories of Hope (10)
Journey of Jesus (12)
The Whole Story - Creation to Redemption (15)
"Follow" - Discover Discipleship (10)
Going "All In" (11)
Groups Becoming Fellowships (9)
Live in Community with Others (8)
Discover Baptism (5)
Discover Prayer (5)
Identity and Purpose (7)
10 Promises of Comfort (10)
Living with Pain (5)
12 Step – Discover the Higher Power (12)
10 Teachings on Discipleship (10)
How are We to Live? (11)
Re-Engage Jesus (12)
Multiply (4)

The Following 117 Stories You Can Find on www.dbsguide.org/additional-studies
Honor and Shame (26)
Ten Stories of Hope (10)
New Believers (18)
Leading Others to Believe (23)
Discover God (13)
Discover Jesus (15)
Discover the Christian Life (12)